Green Heroes

Brandy!
Please show
the world your
Green Heroes now!

Green Heroes

K-5 TEACHING UNIT: HOW DO YOUNG PEOPLE BECOME ENVIRONMENTAL HEROES?

● ● ●

Johnson & Gove

ISBN-13: 9781544139173
ISBN-10: 1544139179

Table of Contents

Introduction: Green Literacy Thematic Teaching Units

● ● ●

GREEN HEROES IS ONE IN a series of Green Literacy Thematic Teaching Units, organized around the 3 Cycles of Comprehension, explicitly so for grades 3-4, and 5, and beyond. They are aligned to the Common Core State Standards. We model how teachers and students can use these texts and digital media as catalysts for critical dialogues and hopefully action toward earth stewardship. Teachers and students reflect that effective action taken toward educating young people includes how solutions work to change systems, including unjust systems like those of race, class, and gender and use of natural resources.

Here is how we introduced this Series at a district-wide summer meeting. We offered a presentation on ways to bring environmental awareness into K-5 classrooms. Teachers discussed two questions: *How do we as educators bring critical environmental issues into our classrooms? What holds us back from adding deep discussions about environmental challenges?*

After we requested their permission to record them, teachers shared their thoughts and feelings. Many teachers talked about their successes, such as thriving school-community gardens, school recycling programs, and nature-based field trips to a zoo or a local nature center. Others spoke about their willingness to raise young people's environmental consciousness, but were uncertain how to go about it. During this presentation, what struck us was the intention to take care of the living world, and, as teachers, sincere willingness to facilitate similar connections for students. Later, as we, the authors, culled the recorded dialogue, we found that even though there is teacher support for student environmental awareness, teachers face concerns, reasonable doubts and significant challenges trying to birth those connections. Teachers shared the following challenges of teaching environmental issues in their classroom.

Rachel: I teach fourth grade. For me, this year is all about getting ready for standardized testing. I see the need for my students to get involved with environmental issues but I need to focus on literacy and math.

Nick: For me, I teach second grade in the city. The neighborhood is a little dangerous so our school doesn't have a garden. We don't go outside much. What I need are ways that I can engage my urban students in environmental issues that are in the classroom and relate to their city life.

Sharia: Environmental issues are huge and scary. They are messy. I don't even know how to bring up something like climate change except in a superficial way. My students recycle. My students turn off the lights, but really, how do you start a deeper conversation? I feel like if I had a way to use something familiar with my fifth grade students and me, it would be more doable.

Henry: I've got a big concern. I want to talk about environmental problems with my students. But the environment and problems like fracking have become so politicized in the news that I am a bit afraid to do so. Is there a way I can start this conversation so that it won't push the buttons of parents who have economic concerns?

Aziza: There are so many demands placed on me as a classroom teacher. I really believe in my third graders thinking about the environment. We created a classroom garden last year. And that's great, but I want to start something where my students think deeper, but I don't know if I have the time or know how to do it. If there was a way to add to what I am doing now, I might be interested in trying it.

Talking with these eco-friendly teachers, we recognized their thoughts and feelings. We felt them, too. Many times, we grappled with our fears, concerns and doubts about teaching controversial environmental issues. Some years, our students made great strides. Other years, we made mistakes that hindered eco-awareness. Throughout our experiences, we valued our classroom time where young people had space to develop their voice and vision on complex environmental situations.

Most importantly, we knew what we felt and experienced about bringing environmental issues into the class was something other teachers, like us, were working toward. From this place of shared concern, we began to explore formal ways of making a bridge between environmental awareness, literacy and empowering young people. Through a decade-long process, we formulated and refined our bridge, which we call *Green Literacy*, a literacy-based practice anchored in our relationship with the earth and humanity, rooted in environmental justice and stemming from Critical Pedagogy.

We coined the term "Green Literacy" after many years of classroom teaching and working with language arts teachers and students from various backgrounds, in both rural and urban areas, public and private schools.

> *Green Literacy is a practice of teaching that develops in-depth thinking, dialoging, and responding to our relationship to the environment using multiple texts and digital media as catalysts.*

Going into the different grade classrooms of K-5, we found that most language arts teachers felt confident in teaching literacy skills using Green Literacy's suggested readings and viewings within a cross curriculum, often using practices of Green Literacy as part of their social studies curriculum. We encountered teachers applying language arts and social studies objectives in Green Literacy teaching. Coming from a literacy-based subject area, teachers wanted to implement the literacy skills of their students to investigate environmental issues through familiar literature and non-fiction formats, but some felt less assured about teaching scientific principles, including those in ecology and the natural sciences. These teachers considered what happens to the environment as imperative to student learning and wanted to use empowering literacy skills to talk about the environment.

We, as authors, value environmental education with its focus on teaching ecological science and its outgrowth of student excursions in nature. We believe that meaningful interactions with the living world often lead to student-initiated earth stewardship, as does Green Literacy practice. Although we acknowledge the need for students to learn scientific principles, Green Literacy seeks to empower teachers and students through environmental justice.

We use the term "Green" to broadly identify any environmental issue with which teachers and students may grapple. We know that young people recognize that recent media attention to the environment has made "Green" the go-to word to represent the environment, and therefore we have used "Green" as a way for teachers and students to recognize that the word has connotations for environmental empowerment.

Green Literacy Thematic Teaching Units in these Series are fixed in Critical Pedagogy so that students examine social context of environmental justice issues, which include race, class, and gender. We created Green Literacy teaching units thematically so that students master how to use evidence and facts to support their assertions and provide teachers with interdisciplinary ties to social studies, science, and other content areas.

Our readers are supported with commentaries that reinforce taking a critical stance concerning environmental themes and books and can venture into several innovative Thematic Teaching Units. Through experimenting with these carefully crafted Thematic Teaching Units, you may use your own creativity to come up with similar units, which will lead to critical thinking, talking, and responding.

Green Literacy Thematic Units use a tool we developed called 3 Cycles of Comprehension, which align with the Common Core State Standards. With the 3 Cycles of Comprehension, readers progress through knowing what the author wrote, supporting their ideas about the text, and entering into critical perspective taking and systemic thinking. These 3 Cycles of Comprehension advance young people's critical thinking, talking and responding, and are tools for teachers to develop their own powerful Green Literacy Thematic Teaching Units.

There is no right way to read each of the Series of *Green Literacy Thematic Teaching Units.* We hope that as you take this journey of considering the themes brought to light in various texts and digital media, conversations will be fueled. Through these experiences we hope you will facilitate opportunities for our young people to make sustainable changes in our communities and the world at large.

In Green Literacy practice, young people interact with text and digital media and engage deeply in the issues through conversations, role-play, Readers' Theatre, and other literacy-based perspective-changing activities that are expected to lead young people to actions toward earth stewardship.

Green Literacy is not synonymous with character education or something teachers do during part of the school day, say in the literacy block or on Earth Day. Green Literacy is done daily when young people strive to unpack power relations in text and media as they relate to environmental justice. Green Literacy develops practices that assist readers to unlock and encounter meaning from text, as well as to understand what texts are doing to the reader and what the author of the text wants the reader to believe about the world, including humans' interactions with the natural world. We believe authors and readers are influential people who have the capacity to perpetuate or challenge particular perceptions of the world, including issues of environmental justice.

SHIFT IN PERSPECTIVE

Our goal in developing *Green Literacy Thematic Teaching Units:* s to impact young people's perspective. As classroom teachers in urban areas, we have witnessed young people participate in Green Literacy practice and amplify their point of view. In the picture book, *Duck! Rabbit!* author Amy Krouse Rosenthal invites the readers to decide if the image on the page is a duck or a rabbit. She uses the lure of optical illusion to reel in the reader's curiosity. *Is this a duck? Is this a rabbit?* The reader shifts her perspective and the images change. Yet when the reader pulls back, she can see the image is both a duck and a rabbit. This is true with environmental issues.

We see teachers and young people developing a continuing shift in view, a magnification of thought, a deeper compassion for the natural world, an ability to grasp and respect our connections to each other and all living things. We believe future generations will need to have the ability to see many sides and the big picture if they want to solve environmental justice challenges.

We envision Green Literacy Thematic Teaching Units as a tool for students and teachers who want to deeply engage in environmental challenges presented within the familiar format of children's books and digital media as springboards for critical thinking and critical dialogue.

We view the practices found within each of these Series as a portal of empowerment for young people to cultivate their own voice, articulate the voices of others, and through this process, be able to create their own critical stance on social justice environmental issues that affect the world they live in.

We believe that the state of our planet depends on how people, including young people and their teachers, as part of a global society of concerned citizens shift perspectives, so that through student-initiated projects, small and large, teachers and their students can contribute to sustainability though systemic change.

We stand for a certain type of teaching, one that facilitates an open and non-authoritative stance, on the part of both you the teacher and your students, and questions power relations. We truly believe that in order to bring about systematic change, first we must have a safe space and abundant time to connect with others where all voices are heard and examined, in creative and deep ways over time.

We hope while using this Thematic Teaching Units, you will take the models presented and create your own thematic units so that environmental challenges within your school-community are used in ways to create student-driven actions. These challenges may be local or global by using the interconnected world of the Internet.

Most fundamentally, our readers are supported with commentaries that reinforce taking a critical stance concerning environmental themes and books and can venture into several innovative Thematic Teaching Units. Through experimenting with these carefully crafted Thematic Teaching Units, you may use your own creativity to come up with similar units, which will lead to critical thinking, talking, and responding. There is no right way to read each *Green Literacy Series or Thematic Teaching Units*. We hope that as you take this journey of considering themes brought to light in various texts and digital media, conversations will be fueled, and that through these experiences young people may one day make sustainable changes in their community and the world at large.

Most importantly, *we thank* our young people and teachers, past, present and future, who work to protect our natural world. We thank them for engaging in practices within this Series of Thematic Teaching Units so young people engage in critical thinking and dialogue. We are grateful for compassionate teachers who guide young people so that community and unity arise, making way for empowering acts of earth stewardship. Our young people are the gatekeepers of our living world and in that respect we offer you, their teachers, practices for them to engage in environmental conversations that will be at the heart of their adult life.

Creating a Green Literacy Classroom

● ● ●

In the end we will conserve only what we love;
we will love only what we understand
and we will understand only what we are taught.

-BABE DIOUM, SENEGALESE POET

GREEN HEROES THEMATIC TEACHING UNITS are part of Green Literacy. We introduce Green Literacy practices for critical reading and speaking that are the foundation of creating a Green Literacy classroom, with a first grade classroom vignette of teacher, Patty, and her Somalis ELL students. To begin, Patty chose the picture book *Where the Forest Meets the Sea* by Jeannie Baker (1988) to read aloud. In Baker's book, a boy and his father explore a primeval forest threatened by commercial development. The father journeys with his son to a remote island reached only by boat. The boy begins to investigate the forest. He follows a creek as it winds through the trees and observes many trees, plants, and animals where all co-exist within the forest peacefully. When the boy returns, his father rests by a fire cooking a freshly caught fish for their evening meal. In the last pages, the boy and his father build a sand castle by the shore. A mirage of a hotel-like resort is partially drawn on the landscape, prompting the reader to consider the future of the primeval forest, a natural resource for the community, and a special place for father and son.

After reading the book aloud, Patty went back and pointed to one page in the book where it says, *My father says there has been a forest there for over a hundred million years* (no page number).

"That sure is a long time this forest has been standing," Patty said. "I want to tell you a word that means a very old forest such as this; it is *primeval.* Let's write it here on our white board."

Patty continued and asked, "What do you think the author means when the boy asked his father, 'but will the forest still be here when we come back?'" (Baker, 1988, no page number).

Maahir raised his hand. "People cut trees to build hotel and park. Maybe when they come back it will be gone. I hope it's not gone."

"Why do you hope the forest is not gone?" Patty prodded.

"There would be no place for them to go," Maahir answered. "And that's sad."

"Look!" Amir said, pointing to the illustration of the mirage at the edge of the page. "What's that?"

"A hotel," Marie said. "And in hotels you can have a job."

"My mother says people make a lot of money when they build big buildings," Dhuuxo said.

"But if more buildings are builded, can the boy and his father get to come back there to camp?" wondered Maahir.

"Good question," Patty said. "Do we all need a place in nature to go as the boy and his father did?"

Several agreed and then spoke about their special nature places.

"I like to play on the beach."

"My auntie brings me to the park where I can climb a tree."

At the class discussion's end, Patty wrote on the board two sentences. *We need jobs. We need a special place in nature.* The first graders then wrote about these two contrasting ideas: having a special place in nature and the need for jobs. Many of the students wrote about their special nature places. A few wrote about their fathers' and mothers' jobs. A couple of students, including Fartuum, attempted to find a solution between nature preservation and economic growth. Fartuum suggested, "We can have jobs at the beach and enjoy being on the beach doing our jobs."

"Good work! Do you think we should make a Green Literacy Ideal about special places in nature?" Patty asked. "What should we say?"

Several students hesitated and waited for more cues from Patty.

"Let's see," Patty said, walking over to the classroom's Green Literacy Ideals. "We already have *We believe everyone should respect nature. We believe we are all connected to all living things.* What can we add?"

"How about *We believe everyone should have a special place to go to in nature*?" Amir said.

To us and to Patty, these first graders dialogued about the dilemma that many feel. Each child voiced the desire for comfort, even luxury; yet at the same time they wanted special places to go in nature. Even though the children and some adults want to be materially secure, many also want to protect and preserve the natural environment.

So how did Patty create a classroom where first graders engaged in this dialogue? How could a teacher of 3rd, 4th, 5th or beyond create a classroom where students participate in deep discussion concerning the environment? How can you use this series to create Green Literacy conversations about the environment? Green Heroes is the first in the Green Literacy Series.

Creating Green Literacy Classrooms is designed to answers these questions, so that you can create a Green Literacy classroom. We demonstrate how Patty supports her students in dialogue as an example practice of K-2 teachers. Then we extend the teaching practice and provide a vignette of a fifth grade teacher, David, leading an extended lesson on *The Boy Who Harnessed the Wind*, including how to develop Green Literacy Ideals, or a shared set of beliefs about the environment. Finally, we discuss Green Literacy's 3 Cycles of Comprehension, made up of literacy best practice, followed by discussions of themes, commentaries, readings and viewings, and thematic teaching units found within Green Heroes.

Now, we explore how K-2 teachers develop comprehension through reading aloud of picture books and viewing digital media to springboard critical conversations about earth stewardship.

DEVELOPING COMPREHENSION, GRADES K-2

The practices found within Green Heroes Thematic Units support all students, even in kindergarten, when the students may be at an emergent reading level. The comprehension skills learned at the K-2 stage translate with continued support over time into thinking critically about texts and multimedia.

A skillful Green Literacy teacher of kindergarten through grade two begins the process of teaching comprehension. At K-2 grade levels and beyond, teachers work together with their students in the comprehension process; they ask their students to provide evidence for why they have their viewpoints about texts; they do not focus on "the one correct answer"; they support students in sharing what they are thinking and feeling.

With the practice of Green Literacy, K-2 teachers' emphasis is on encouraging their students to speak up in classroom discussions with their observations, connections, wonderings, and ideas about illustrations and the way the books and digital media are written and produced. Teachers encourage active comprehension. They ask kindergarteners through second graders to ask questions and make predictions. In this process, students become more goal directed. They listen or read to satisfy the students' own purposes rather than the teacher's. A critical feature of teaching students to actively comprehend while they listen or read is to help them relate their prior knowledge to the content of what they hear or read. Text connections are thought of in three ways: text-to-self, often just called "making a connection," text-to-text, and text-to-world (Keene & Zimmerman, 2007). A text-to-world connection is more inferential and asks students to make a connection beyond the story or nonfiction piece. A first grader's response of the text-to-world connection for *The Giving Tree* is, "The story makes me think of how much trees give us and what we don't give back to them. I think we need to take care of trees, not just take from them."

In some classrooms, when discussions occur, the teacher and/or a few vocal students can quickly dominate them. This is especially true in K- 2 classrooms. In an effort to keep the discussion moving forward, some teachers may ask too many questions too rapidly. Often young children are reticent about participating or becoming involved when discussions are monopolized either by the teacher or by a few students.

We advocate the use of Turn and Talk, particularly in kindergarten through grade 2 classrooms. In this way, every student expresses her thoughts to a classmate and then many ideas are shared with the whole group. Kindergarten through grade 2 teachers can also use a Discussion Web, which has students discuss a question that reflects more than one point of view such as in the book *Where the Red Fern Grows* (Rawls, 1961). The discussion question could be, "Should Billy have cut down the large sycamore tree in order to get the coon?" The Discussion Web strategy includes talking in pairs, then foursomes, and then whole class sharing. This strategy also provides an opportunity for each child to share her ideas.

In *Green Heroes* and the other Green Literacy Series,, we offer a K-2 vignette that uses specific teaching strategies that create meaningful comprehension building routines. Using these routines several times supports the young peoples' ability to become independent. These teaching strategies support K-2 students entering into conversations about environmental challenges. Students support their ideas by drawing from the text or digital media. After the vignette, we provide three or four related picture books and digital media based on the Series' theme that can be used with the same specific strategies. In this way, K-2 graders familiarize themselves with comprehension supporting strategy while partaking in essential urgent environmental conversation of the day.

Building on those K-2 skills is a natural progression toward critical perspective in grades 3, 4, and 5 and beyond, where the 3 Cycles of Comprehension are more explicitly taught during Green Literacy practice.

3 CYCLES OF COMPREHENSION

The 3 Cycles of Comprehension involving Best Practice teaching, well known by teachers, are explicitly taught in grades 3, 4, 5 and beyond. They are grouped in the following way:

DEFINITIONS OF THE 3 CYCLES OF COMPREHENSION

Cycle 1: Simple Comprehension occurs when young people retell or summarize the story/nonfiction text or digital media, including when they make inferences about what the author wrote.

Cycle 2: Criteria Comprehension occurs when young people support their thinking about the story/nonfiction text or digital media with criteria either prompted by the teacher or from their own thinking.

Cycle 3: Critical Perspective Comprehension occurs when young people engage in the story/nonfiction text or digital media that becomes less an end in itself than a doorway through which they explore the social world and their relationship to it. This includes both explicit and implicit perspectives and characters debating different sides of issues, as well as valuing and developing assumptions and beliefs that make sense to the young people. Critical Perspective Comprehension also includes systems thinking, that is, thinking which concerns how one event is related to or is caused by other events and involves solving complex problems.

Now we offer a vignette that shows Green Literacy practice in action in a fifth grade classroom. In this example, David, the teacher, facilitated his class in a more sophisticated and prolonged engagement with environmental complexities, moving his students through the 3 Cycles of Comprehension around the text, *The Boy Who Harnessed the Wind.*

Developing Comprehension Grades 3-5 and Beyond

David is a fifth grade teacher at a school where grades are looped. With David as their fourth grade and now their fifth grade teacher, David's students had experience working in critical thinking groups. David used the biography, *The Boy Who Harnessed the Wind.* In this remarkable biography of a 14-year-old Malawi boy, William Kamkwamba engineered a windmill from what he read in library books. The biography divides William's life into three parts: 1) village life of subsistence farming through child William's eyes, 2) a famine and how William studied elementary physics textbooks in a local library and used scrap materials to build his first windmill, and 3) the outside world discovers William, which leads to him giving a TED talk and eventually going to Dartmouth University. David selected this biography to show how technology impacts developing countries. David wanted his students to consider how the Internet enables people to get information they want and to connect with helpful people beyond the local village or city. William built his first windmill with only an old textbook and without international monetary support. After William made friends at a TED conference, he was able to obtain the resources to go to school and eventually build more windmills for his village. David also led his students to dialogue about how the best international assistance may be rooted in local connections rather than top-down efforts through foreign governments.

As a pre-reading activity and an introduction into Cycle 1 Simple Comprehension, students watched and responded to William Kamkwamba's first TED Talks (2007). Afterwards, they developed questions to use as they read the book. His students came up with the following:

- So he didn't go to school. Why not? Did he ever get to go to school?
- How did he make this windmill? Did anyone help him?
- Did he make the second windmill?

* How did the TED people help him?
* What happened to William after he made the first TED talk?

These questions set the stage for close reading, which is Cycle 1 Simple Comprehension, moving to Cycle 2 Criteria Comprehension. David encouraged his class to read while they worked with partners to cite specifically what happens in each of the three parts of the book, and the partners developed a timeline of events for each part of the book. Afterwards, David started the first of three whole-group discussions. During the first of these whole-group discussions, David focused on Cycle 1 Simple Comprehension and stressed, "Let's discuss what actually happened before we jump to the big ideas." The young people shared their timelines and came to a consensus as they made a master timeline for each of the three parts in the biography.

Once the students had read the entire book, had worked on the timeline in partners, and David was sure all students had mastered Cycle 1 Simple Comprehension, he showed William Kamkwamba's second TED Talk (2009), made two years after his first TED Talk. The students were impressed with William's improved English and confidence. They liked his final message: "I tried and I made it. Trust yourself and believe."

David then moved the young people into Cycle 2 Criteria Comprehension, in which they found support in the text for their ideas. The partners combined the partner groups to form foursomes of experts. With their timelines, each group chose events in the book that demonstrated value or need for one of the following: science, technology—particularly the Internet, and social justice. A week later, when the student groups presented, the listeners used a spider map graphic organizer to link the different areas of expertise.

Moving into Cycle 3 Critical Perspective Comprehension, David asked, "Can anyone share connections between the perspectives? And I dare you to refer to a page in the book."

Ronald, from the science group, raised his hand. "I see social justice and science connected. Before William made the windmill, his family lived on subsistence farming and went through a terrible famine where they only had one scoop of maize porridge each day. I take the dare. Page 74."

Tamara said, "I see technology and activism connect. The activism came from people William met at the TED conference. Plus, after the village realized the windmill could bring them electricity and people from outside came to see the windmill, the whole village was proud of William's accomplishment."

"But how was that activism?" David pushed.

"Well, William met activists from the US at the TED conference and they helped him get money by communicating through the Internet for William's ideas of getting electricity to others in his village, and for William and his friends to be able to go to school, things like that," Tamara answered.

"Why do you think the village people changed their mind about William? How did their perspective change?" David said. "Double dog dare if you provide the page to your idea."

James, a shy student, offered, "They wanted to have electricity too. They saw good things can happen in the village and in other villages. On page 251, William's mother said when she was asked about having lights in her house from her son's work, 'We're proud. But we thought he was going mad.'"

"Good thinking," said David, and then shifted the discussion. "Remember when we talked about different kinds of power? Let's list them." David's students listed power sources such as coal and natural gas, as well as alternative energy sources such as wind and solar. They noted that in Chicago where they lived, their electricity came from power plants fueled by coal. "As we talk, " David continued, "let's consider what thoughts we should write as our Green Literacy Ideals."

In a brief discussion about what they could add to the classroom's Green Literacy Ideals, students talked about how William's windmill helped his family so they could have lights to read by. Plus, the second windmill helped them irrigate their crops, so their life became less difficult. Then Jerome added, "We believe fuel sources, especially alternative energy, are greatly needed and should be shared with developed countries."

"Wow," said David. "This idea is a breakthrough Green Literacy Ideal. Class, do you agree?" The class all raised their hands in agreement.

The discussion continued when Julie said, paraphrasing from the book, "I think that activism from the developed world can help African countries to have more wind and solar power. On page 214 William's father said he enjoys his lights more than a city person because he had paid nothing to the power company and he has no power outages like people in the city. So maybe helping small communities in Africa make windmills for their town like William did might be better than everybody getting electricity from one big giant power plant like how we do here in Chicago."

"Yeah," added Tamara. "Remember what happened to William's town when the grain supplies were sold off by the president's friends? Everyone starved and only a few people had grain to eat."

"So," said Michael, changing the subject, "Wind and solar power are called alternative sources of energy because they are not traditional sources of energy which are mostly from fossil fuels like coal and oil."

"Good use of words, Michael," David said. "Alternative energy is a term on our Green Literacy word wall."

David referred back to what Julie had said earlier. "Julie and class, I like our discussion about local forms of energy and how they helped William's town grow rather than having big companies or governments come in and take over the energy supply. Maybe this idea might be turned into one of our Green Literacy Ideals. What do you think, class, do we believe that local energy sources like wind and solar are a tool to bring energy with some control over it for local people? Is this idea important enough to be one of our Green Literacy Ideals?"

After more discussion the class agreed and David placed this Green Literacy Ideal on the list on their wall: *Small scale local alternative energy sources are extremely helpful to small villages in developing countries because they can acquire them more easily than large scale energy sources.*

Before the bell rang Ronald asked, "What can we do here in Chicago? We've got electricity and rarely have power outages. What can we do to be like William?"

Looking at this vignette through the lens of Green Literacy Practice, David progresses his students through the 3 Cycles of Comprehension. The students mastered Cycle 1 Simple Comprehension when they first determined what the author wrote through reading and working with partners to develop a timeline of what happened in each of the three parts of the book. The students progressed into Cycle 2 Criteria Comprehension when they defended their ideas with information in the text as they worked in expert groups, considering the value or need for science, technology (particularly the Internet), and social justice. Plus, students engaged in complex thought and interpretation in Cycle 3 Critical Perspective Comprehension when the class articulated differing perspectives concerning alternative energy, particularly wind, in developing countries.

Secondly, David and his students created their own Green Literacy Ideals through in-depth discussion concerning "the whys and how's" of alternative energy used in developing countries. In fact, the class came up with and agreed upon two Green Literacy Ideals.

ZEROING IN ON CREATING GREEN LITERACY IDEALS

Green Literacy Ideals are a set of shared values about our relationship with the living world. Collectively, each classroom creates their Green Literacy Ideals through a process of critical discussion and systemic evaluation of environmental themes. To create Green Literacy Ideals, teachers and students must grapple with the 3 Cycles of Comprehension on an environmental theme found within specific texts or digital media. Consider how David and his students as well as Patty and her students created Green Literacy Ideals. Also, we offer a further discussion and our own Green Literacy Ideals in Appendix A. Green Literacy Theory.

THEMATIC TEACHING UNITS

We designed the Green Literacy Thematic Units to create close communities of learners. Working in a close community, according to Moser (2007), is necessary to help individuals stay aware, for such discussions may be easily overwhelming as young people sort through complex issues, understand difficult trade-offs, and change habitual thoughts and behaviors—all of which are part of solving most environmental issues. Typically, interpersonal and small-group dialogue addresses these needs much better than mass communication like radio or television. In each of the Green Literacy Series, we offer thematic teaching units that create this sense of community.

Equally important, we recommend grade levels at which the specific books and digital media in the teaching units can be used. This is a guideline. Teachers know their students and are aware of their preferences, which helps them determine what books should be read. This partiality needs to be considered as much as our grade level recommendations.

Further, as a way of summarizing what Green Literacy students do as they work through Green Literacy's 3 Cycles of Comprehension, we developed the following characteristics of a Green Literacy K-5 thinker and reader, which we call "Comprehenders."

CHARACTERISTICS OF K-5 GREEN LITERACY "COMPREHENDERS"

* Interacts/ engages with certain books and digital media which function as springboards for vital discussions about environmental stewardship that probably would not occur otherwise, since

environmental issues are complex, interconnected, and often cloaked in another problem.

Example: "I never thought about how a big storm could affect us before and how we are all connected, " said fourth grader James in a discussion about *I Survived Katrina* by Lauren Tarshis.

* Understands that most young people in the developed world will increase an awareness of environmental and social justice unfairness and their part in the system that perpetuates environmental and social justice unfairness.

Example: *"The Story of Stuff* made me think about how my getting a new cell phone every two years may not be such a great idea in the big picture. Can you imagine how many cell phones there will be in 10 years?" said fifth grader Kirk.

* Appreciates that facts and points of view will be accumulated through reading, viewing, and discussing.

Example: "Wow, look at the Green Literacy Ideals we wrote throughout the school year about sharing water. I never realized how many sides there are to water rights," observed Janice, a third grader.

- Recognizes that diverging sources of information reinforce such facts and points of view and actively applies how to check the credibility of sources.

Example: After reading *Flash Point* by Sneed B. Collard, fourth grader Pedro started thinking about why there are so many wildfires in the West. "I googled wildfires and loggers. I found out that American Loggers Council wants to pass a law for land management — cutting down trees — saying it would decrease fires. I wonder how credible this idea is?"

- Respects that everyone has a right to his/her opinion; values multiple perspectives on an environmental issue, supporting thinking deeply and critically.

Example: While discussing animal rights, third grader Carlos said, "I respect people who are vegetarians because that is their choice. My family eats meat. That is our choice."

- Realizes how complex systems interact and ways to change them systemically, including the power dynamics needed to make system changes, and how students can work with others to make needed systemic changes.

Example: Fifth grader Helen said, "*She's Wearing A Dead Bird on Her Head!* (Lasky) made me think about how women wearing birds on their heads hurt both the birds *and* the women, making them look ridiculous, and hurt women's suffrage prospects. Minna and Harriet and their husbands worked to change's women's tastes of hats and to change laws to protect birds and for women to vote."

We know that low, middle, and high readability level students mix and mingle their ideas during critical discussions around big ideas. When students return to individual work, they have richer background knowledge. Students participate in a combination of read-alouds, silent reading, and multimedia formats followed by critical discussion. Implementing these critical discussions levels the playing field for students who struggle with word recognition and reading fluency. Often low-readability readers are the students who are able to "think outside of the box" during a discussion. As students move through the 3 Cycles of Comprehension, teachers may increase student readability levels.

GREEN LITERACY THEMES

We believe when teachers and students are involved in environmental themes where students generate critical dialogue and thinking, many times students will initiate action around local or global environmental issues in which they become personally invested. For example, in Series Two, we present the theme of how extreme weather events in the past affected us and how we will respond to them in the future. Based on the theme, each class will create its own critical discussions that are unique to their geographic area. If one lives near New Orleans or New Jersey, the class is likely to discuss Hurricane Katrina or Sandy respectively. Discussions concerning what to do about hurricanes in the future are likely to bring forth discussions around such ideas as how to build natural protection for rising sea levels. In Ohio, Arkansas, and Oklahoma, recent small earthquakes near hydraulic fracking waste injection wells may be the severe weather events discussed. In California the dialogue may move to drought and conserving water. In all locations, climate change, sometimes now called climate chaos, may be a part of the conversation.

We offer multi-grade themes, as do many inquiry-based learning curricula such as the International Baccalaureate curriculum. This approach provides students the opportunity to consider local and global issues that are age/grade appropriate and does not confine learning into subject areas, that is, it is interdisciplinary. Since the themes are significant, students at the differing grade levels inquire into, and learn about, these globally significant issues in the context of Thematic Units, each of which addresses a central idea relevant to a particular theme. Multiple texts and media, recommended for differing grade levels, act as springboards to in-depth dialogue. These texts and media are identified in order to explore the scope of the central idea for each Thematic Teaching Unit at specific grade levels. Then, these overarching themes are explored again at increasingly higher grade levels, where more sophisticated critical thinking occurs. These Thematic Teaching Units are substantial, in-depth, and usually last for several weeks.

Our themes highlight concerns within the environmental movement with a focus on humanity's interaction with nature. All of the themes have a relationship to environmental justice. We believe the definition provided by the Environmental Protection Agency (EPA) aligns with Green Literacy. The EPA defines environmental justice as "the fair treatment and meaningful involvement of all people regardless of race, color, national origin, or income with respect to the development, implementation, and enforcement of environmental laws, regulations, and policies. EPA has this goal for all communities and persons across this Nation [sic]. It will be achieved when everyone enjoys the same degree of protection from environmental and health hazards and equal access to the decision-making process to have a healthy environment in which to live, learn, and work" (EPA website).

We embrace the EPA definition of environmental justice that everyone should enjoy the same degree of protection from environmental and health hazards and equal access to the decision-making process to have a healthy environment in which to live, learn, and work. We believe that for citizens to have access to the decision-making process, they need to be able to take a critical stance in relationship to earth stewardship with all its complexity. To us, earth stewardship is intertwined with and of equal importance to social justice. Issues such as pollution, deterioration of the physical condition of communities, as well as access to natural resources and renewable energy are part of public discourse. As that discourse grows, young people become increasingly aware of the larger-scale environmental problems and their connection to social justice. Young people can and should be *connected to* and find *their voice in* the on-going conversation. They find their voice by taking a critical stance on environmental issues through engaging in Green Literacy's themes.

We offer the following inquiry-based themes:

- Series One: How do Young People Become Green Heroes?
- Series Two: How Does Landscape Impact Our Identities?
- Series Three: How Does Extreme Weather Shape Our Communities?
- Series Four: How can We Cultivate Sustainable Change through Systemic Thinking?

GREEN LITERACY COMMENTARY

Green Literacy Commentary is a series of interpretations about an environmental theme that poses questions that often disrupt what is commonly assumed, investigates the credibility of writers and producers, and evaluates power relationships and the complexity of systemic thinking surrounding environmental dilemmas.

Our experiences working with teachers and students have shown us that teachers become more engaged with environmental themes and their complexity when they have access to supporting commentaries. We define commentary as a series of interpretations about an environmental theme that poses questions, which often disrupt what is commonly assumed. Our commentaries question the credibility of what writers write and producers produce. We examine power relationships, leadership issues, and solutions that advocate systemic thinking. Our commentaries draw from sociology, ecology, and natural history. They reflect a critical stance, which can include eco-criticism.

The purpose of our commentaries found in each of the series is to support teachers' thinking before they teach, while they teach, and when they reflect upon their teaching of a Green Literacy Thematic Teaching Unit. We supply commentaries because we believe that teachers must explore a deeper level of thinking in order to move their students into considering viable possibilities that meet our environmental challenges and heal our relationship with the earth. We offer Green Literacy commentaries for teachers in similar fashion to the way Green Literacy teachers provide for young people Green Literacy texts and digital media to springboard a critical stance. Our commentaries supply rich background by asking questions that show a way of thinking emphasized by critical literacy theorists such as Shor.

Our experience indicates that teachers and students need time, space, and effort to look critically and deeply at environmental issues. They need reflection and ongoing conversations with other teachers and subject experts. Thus, we offer the commentaries to push a teacher's critical thinking as well as instill confidence in the teacher to launch into these conversations with young people.

Through our commentary we aim to widen the context so that the text is meaningful to students (Knapp, 1995). Through the 3 Cycles of Comprehension and the teacher support of commentaries, students travel beyond what the author conveys and toward points of view of those not mentioned in the text (Luke, Comber, & O'Brien, 1996). The possibility of transformation toward a more just, equitable, and tolerant society empowers young people and motivates them to acquire and apply reading and writing skills to articulate their ideas.

We provide two kinds of commentaries for teachers within each of the series. At the beginning of each of the series we provide commentary on the overarching environmental theme. For instance, in the opening commentary of Series Two, we discuss the theme of valuing place. By becoming familiar and comfortable with details of a particular landscape, be it urban fringe or widespread suburbia, teachers and their students explore how they identify and associate with certain places, and together develop compassion and understanding toward the spaces in which they live and consider the empowerment of stewardship within their local landscape.

Second, throughout the Green Literacy Series,, we offer commentaries on the environmental theme of singular text or digital media. For example, Series Two's theme is *How does landscape impact our identities?* One of the books, we feature is *Wild Wing* (2011), written by Gill Lewis. The commentary in this Series builds an awareness of how an injured, tagged osprey migrates from Scotland to Africa and brings together people who are connected to each of these places. Both types of commentary, the one at the start of *Green Heroes* and the other about specific text or digital media within *Green Heroes*, buoys teachers and their students to think about and formulate a critical stance, which is essential to partaking in environmental justice.

In order to illustrate how our commentaries support teachers, we offer a sample, which is exemplary of the ones found in each of the Green Literacy Series. This example of our commentaries is about a single text, Molly Bang's picture book, *Common Ground: Earth and Air We Share*. We chose this example because even though *Common Ground* is a singular book, the theme is comprehensive and focuses on common natural resources that are shared by many and often polluted by a few. We provide context with a 3rd grade vignette on the environmental theme and book, *Common Ground*, showing how Albert, the teacher, used this commentary with his classroom.

Commentary on *Common Ground*
Common Ground: The Water, Earth, and Air We Share by Molly Bang (1997) gives credit for the inspiration for the

book to Garrett Hardin's seminal paper, "The Tragedy of the Commons," published in *Science* magazine in 1968. Hardin's paper puts forth in a striking manner the problem faced by a group of New England landowners in managing the town commons. The commons provided grazing land for each landowner's sheep, but the number of sheep grazed needed to be limited or the grass would be ruined, destroying it for future use. As it is in the interest of each property owner to graze as many sheep as possible, the result if the dilemma is unresolved will lead to the "tragedy" of the destruction of the common resource. Drawing from this "big idea" of Hardin's, the picture book *Common Ground* introduces young readers to this concept of the commons, which is so central to our environmental dilemmas.

Through illustration and text, the book begins with the idea of the New England landowners sharing grazing land. *Common Ground* then uses this concept to demonstrate how people and businesses benefit from the easy availability of oil, gas, and coal as fuel and to make products, and the seeming abundance of water for all our needs, at least "in the short run." Bang then writes:

> But someday, these fossil fuels will be used up . . . over time, the wells run dry, and the wastes pollute the water. There is not enough clean water for all the people, the farms, and the businesses. Fresh water, fossil fuels, forest, fish— one by one, we are destroying the natural resources that sustain our lives.

The book shows how *the water, earth, and air we share* are endangered, and unless the predicament of overuse of these environmental resources is resolved by society, they will no longer be available. We think a good question that propels critical thinking concerning this issue is *What should we keep and preserve for the common good and what should be made private and for profit?* Each person, rich and poor, needs air to breathe, water to drink and bathe, food to eat, and some form of energy to move about. For example, consider, can someone own the air we all breathe? Can anyone fish in the ocean or should someone own it?

Using this commentary about *Common Ground* as support, a third-grade inclusion teacher, Albert, began to think about ways to engage his students in understanding the big-picture idea of the commons. Since he was not an environmental scientist, nor had he much experience with teaching the concept of the commons, this commentary instilled in him a confidence to begin teaching about the commons to his students. After reading the commentary, Albert was motivated to do his own research on the topic of the commons. He found Hardin's scientific paper, which he found difficult to read, but was captivated by reviews of Hardin's thoughts. After considering the importance of the idea of the commons, Albert located and mapped out local examples of commons near his school such as a park and the public school he taught in, so he could share with students. Albert contemplated what he thought as appropriate to have as common spaces and other spaces to have private.

For example, Albert recognized a nearby lake was used in common for swimming and boating, even for his community's water supply. He also thought about how he and his family owned their home on the lake, which included private beach access.

How did Albert incorporate the Green Literacy Commentary into his teaching of the book *Common Ground*? How did his students gain understanding of common ground through the classroom discussions? We follow the thinking of one student, Mia.

Exploring the Commons in a 3rd Grade Vignette

Before reading the book *Common Ground: The Water, Earth, and Air We Share* by Molly Bang aloud to his students, Albert wanted them to be aware of the concept of common ground; he planned two consecutive days for discussion before reading the book aloud. During the first discussion, the students wavered in their understanding about common ground and the importance of preserving their environment. Many could not articulate what common ground looked like. One student, Mia, commented that common ground belonged "everywhere but nowhere." Along with the rest of her classmates, she had heard the word pollution and said, "smoking stinks!" but did not connect how pollution played a big factor in her urban life or in the preservation of the commons. The second day's discussion began with brainstorming things that could be shared in their homes, their classroom, their school, and their neighborhoods. Mia offered several suggestions, including shared sidewalks, and in her case a shared courtyard at her apartment complex. While students came up with examples of shared resources, Albert emphasized the idea of sharing and supporting resources for the *common ground*. The concept began to click in the students' minds. They could understand the need for a shared, common supply of pencils available when a student needed one. With Albert's guidance, the students came up with other examples of sharing toys and books as well as the streets and drinking fountains outside. Mia came up with the idea that "Common Ground must be like a park. Everyone can go there and no one owns it." For the third and final day's discussion Albert read aloud *Common Ground: The Water, Earth, and Air We Share*. The class debated the importance of taking care of their shared or common environment, and the implications of pollution in their homes, classrooms, and school. Another discussion took place. This time Mia remembered being at the park where a strong smell came from water in a small pond. The water was green and slimy. "That pond isn't for the common good! Nobody can use it!" Mia's response led the way for other students to consider how commons can be polluted by the few while affecting the many.

After the discussion, Albert asked them to come up with ideas to preserve the commons in their school. Students came up with concepts like putting up a "No Littering" sign in the cafeteria to preserve their dining environment for the *common good*. The students also decided to talk to the school principal before putting up the sign in the cafeteria and received her support; in this way they worked with the school's power structure. So, the commentary on the book *Common Ground* empowered Albert to move his third graders to consider the importance of the commons and to take action by working with the school's power structure. This kind of action taken by Albert's students is an outgrowth of a Green Literacy dialogue that we the authors of this book hope will occur.

Green Literacy Suggested Readings and Viewings

Green Literacy readings and viewings is an on-going collection of children's books and digital media whose themes draw on how humans interact with the natural world.

Books like *Common Ground* were chosen to be included in the Green Literacy suggested readings, in each of the Series and at our companion website, GreenLiteracy.org, for their accessibility and range, their resonant similarities, and their illuminating differences, and most importantly for the connections they make between humanity and nature. *Common Ground* and many similar books are annotated on our companion website, GreenLiteracy.org, which is continually updated. We also included digital media as classrooms integrate more innovative technology into their multi-grade curriculum. Our selected digital media offers opportunities similar to those found in books in selections where students connect, think critically, and provide springboards for student dialogue. We recognize that as more people embrace earth stewardship, more publications and digital media will arise.

On our companion website, GreenLiteracy.org, we offer hundreds of books and digital media choices for teachers and students to consider when they create their own Green Literacy Thematic Teaching Units or would like to add to their environmental justice school and classroom library to deepen individual student learning. In addition, we actively invite and encourage readers to contribute their own meaningful suggestions.

At present, our decision for a selection's inclusion within the Green Literacy Suggested Readings and Viewings was based on the following questions:

Does the book or digital media
(1) express a connection to humanity and the environment?
(2) require students to use critical thinking when reading for an environmental justice-themed story or nonfiction?
(3) enable students to provide multiple answers and perspectives to the environmental justice- themed story or digital media's situation?
(4) have the possibility of students connecting personally to the environmental justice-themed stories

and to their local or global landscape in hopes of eventual action towards earth stewardship?

Looking through Green Heroes and on the search engines on GreenLiteracy.org, readers will find that many of the books within Green Literacy's suggested readings and viewing have a prominent place in class, school, and neighborhood libraries. Some older classics like *The Giving Tree* (1964) by Shel Silverstein and *The Lorax* (1971) by Dr. Seuss continue in print, plus the numbers of books published with similar themes are growing. For example, some picture books focus on how humans work with nature, such as the funny picture book, *How the Ladies Stopped the Wind* by Bruce McMillan (2007), which sparks young people in discussing their experiences of living in harsh weather, such as sandbagging overflowing rivers or growing plants by keeping wildlife such as deer from eating newly-formed leaves. Students explore how green gardens aid in rejuvenation of the local green economy in their big city, and a systemic way for communities to work both with nature and the economy.

Other examples within Green Literacy's suggested readings are Laurie Lawlor's biography titled *Rachel Carson and Her Book that Changed the World* (2012) and Lynne Cherry's illustrated *The Sea, the Storm, and the Mangrove Tangle* (2004), a hybrid with information on ecology within a fictional story. These books answer our four questions by emphasizing human interaction with nature and the threat posed to nature by human activity: in *Rachel Carson*, the threat of chemicals to bird life; and in *The Sea, the Storm, and the Mangrove Tangle*, the impact of pollution and development on mangrove ecology. Lawlor also mentions how chemical companies protected their interests and tried to discredit Carson and her pioneering book, *Silent Spring* (1962).

The Green Literacy Suggested Readings continues to grow and includes other recent books, such as *Awesome Dawson* by Chris Gall (2013), who collects other people's junk and makes it into something stupendous, as well as *Forest, What Would You Like?* by Irene O'Garden (2013), a poem considering the forest's perspective, written with 400 children's responses. A middle-grade book, *Mousemobile* by Prudence Breitrose (2013), also qualifies for the Green Literacy reading, for *Mousemobile* features young people who work for some super-smart mice combating global warming; this fantasy activates critical thinking about this phenomena.

We acknowledge the importance of informational science texts. These nonfiction content books are essential to young people's interpretation of the natural world and are an important part of the science curriculum. Such examples include Anne Rockwell's *Why Are the Ice Caps Melting?* (2006), which introduces young readers to the facts about climate change but not the human interactions around it. Another example of an informational science text is *And Then There Was One* by Margaret Facklam (1993), which familiarizes readers with animal extinction, and again offers data but not human connection. However, these books do not answer our four questions. In effect, they do not address the human factor within complex environmental issues, which is the reason we developed Green Literacy.

The Green Literacy suggested readings and viewings along with traditional nonfiction science content books are useful for frontloading and concept gathering and in turn align themselves with the Common Core State Standards. Thus students handling both Green Literacy and science content texts learn to cite from the source and formulate argumentative writing. Reading, viewing, and interacting with selections from Green Literacy's suggestions are best integrated with environmental science books and digital media, and if possible used in conjunction with excursions into nature where students experience their local environment.

Digital Media
Digital media utilizes information and interaction in different ways. To use digital media, young people must know how to use a wide range of related features, such as how to read for understanding, compose messages, navigate nonlinear text, infer meaning, and repeatedly critically evaluate the credibility of digital texts/images. Teachers use similar practices such as viewing the digital beforehand, drawing out connections between what is seen and what is read, as

well as integrating meaningful digital media into the teaching units.

We see digital media in the Green Literacy suggestions as serving a distinct purpose. From our experiences as teachers in different types of schools, we have found that digital media levels the playing field. It allows students to experience viewing individually yet collectively. Many times, students with low readability levels are able to connect with a visual rendering of information and story and are able to enrich their background knowledge so that when they do see similar material in written form, they have more capacity for comprehension. Also important, these same students can contribute to a classroom dialogue based on their viewing, which serves to increase confidence and create a critical stance.

An example of digital media in the Green Literacy suggestion is a short video clip called *Message in Waves*, in which Meghan talks about the place she lives called Midway, located in Northwestern Hawaiian Islands. During World War II, Midway was a naval air station and submarine base. Now nearly two million birds of 19 species nest on Midway, and among them is the largest colony of Laysan albatrosses in the world. *Message in Waves* serves as a way for students to talk about how our human consumption of plastic bottles interferes with nesting grounds. Another example we offer is a short, animated video clip called *Biofuels* from the popular website BrainPop. In *Biofuels*, students view how burning fossil fuels emits gases that lead to pollution and global climate change and how scientists and engineers are developing new fuels that are completely renewable and much healthier for the environment. Both of the digital media examples adhere to the four questions and spark critical dialogue, helping students to formulate a critical stance.

GREEN LITERACY THEMATIC TEACHING UNITS

Each Green Literacy Series or Thematic Teaching Unit is a cluster of several lessons that conceptually fit together around an environmental theme. They are multi-grade, with specific books and media recommended for differing grade levels.

We offer in *Green Heroes Series* dynamic teaching units that model how Green Literacy works in the classroom through actual classroom examples, teacher-student dialogues, and teacher-teacher conversations. Our experience shows that once teachers have engaged their students and themselves in several of the thematic teaching units found in *Green Literacy Series*, they acquire a sense of how to create their own Green Literacy Thematic Teaching Units, and are inspired to do so.

The Thematic Teaching Units in the Green Literacy Series draw on multiple texts and digital media with the same theme; they creatively use reading and writing strategies that lead to environmental and social critique in recommended grade level ranges. Green Literacy teachers and young people gain confidence and insight needed to skillfully interact in multiple Best Practice literacy strategies such as Readers' Theatre, Directed Reading Thinking Activity, Free Response, Making Connections and so on. In each of the Green Literacy Series and for specific books and digital media as well as by grade level, we offer learning activities aligned with Common Core State Standards. For example, in Green Heroes students can engage in such strategies as Readers' Theatre, Think Pair Share and Intra Act.

We advocate a thematic approach as outlined in International Baccalaureate and other 21st century curricula as well as the Common Core State Standards. We recognize that kindergarten students are different from fifth graders and that there is a need to identify grade levels as they correspond with CCSS. Green Literacy is geared toward kindergarten to 5th grade students. We believe the concepts and applications provided will allow students and their teachers to move comprehension skills from direct instruction to guided practice, to independent critical perspective thinking, that is, scaffolding the teaching toward developing an independent learner as suggested in CCSS (Coleman, & Pimentel, 2012). We believe that the practice of Green Literacy is appropriate beyond 5th grade. We have engaged adults in Green Literacy practice by beginning scintillating, productive conversations using children's literature and media that foreground a complex environmental issue.

How to Use *Green Literacy Series*

We offer guidelines on How to Use *Green Literacy Series.* The first set of guidelines is the structural setup of each of the Series and details how differentiating grade level teachers can approach the learning activities and commentaries. The second set of guidelines comprises Appendices concerning Common Core State Standards, correlation with International Baccalaureate curriculum, and assessment.

Structural Setup: What's Inside Green Heroes

The structural setup for each of the Series is the same throughout, so that as you familiarize yourself with Green Heroes, you can refer quickly to what interests you and your students.

Each Series centers on a specific environmental inquiry based theme. We open with commentary about the theme, drawing from various sources, such as sociology, history, ecology and social justice.

The K-2 classroom vignette serves as a model of teaching to support comprehension and is aligned to the CCSS. We end with suggestions of other books and digital media that could be used with the teaching strategies.

We move into the sections suggested for grades 3-5 and beyond. The two sections are organized by suggested grade levels: Grades 3-4, and Grades 4- 5 & Beyond.

Each of these sections includes:

- Three theme-related texts or digital media with commentaries.
- Lessons based on the 3 Cycles of Comprehension with best practice strategies, aligned to CSS with student activities on how these texts fit together thematically.
- Suggestions of other books and digital media that could be used with the teaching strategies and theme.

We end each Green Literacy Series with a section called *Investigate and Connect Through Writing*, which explores environmental justice issues through writing and credible sources for students to use for inquiry into topics related to each Series' theme, aligned with Common Core Standards. Projects initiated by young people are also explored and encouraged.

READER CIRCUMSTANCES
If you are interested in our process in developing the Thematic Teaching Units, , we invite readers into our thinking process on how we developed the Thematic Teaching Units. We include this so that readers can begin their own thinking processes to create Thematic Teaching Units that best benefit their students and schools. We hope that as you design Thematic Teaching Units, you and your students become emboldened by your local and global connections

to environmental challenges and that you carry out student-initiated action.

Also we created three appendices that speak to various reader circumstances. They can be found at the end of each of the Series. Our appendices are meant to be guides. We hope that readers will encounter what fits their students' needs.

THEORY FOCUS: APPENDIX A. GREEN LITERACY THEORY

Read this Appendix if you are interested in the theory behind how to support students in taking a critical stance, drawn from critical pedagogy, or if you want you to explore such theorists as Freire, Shor and Shannon. We explain Green Literacy Ideals and their importance. We also provide an in-depth look at the Three Cycles of Comprehension in this Appendix. We also offer classroom research on facilitating critical dialogue.

COMMON CORE STATE STANDARD FOCUS: APPENDIX B. COMMON CORE STATE STANDARDS IN GREEN LITERACY PRACTICE.

If you and/or your district is involved in Common Core State Standards (CCSS), you will find our ideas about CCSS and Green Literacy practice as well as the full (not abbreviated), aligned CCSS standards for the K-5 teaching activities in each of the Green Literacy Series.

INTERNATIONAL BACCALAUREATE FOCUS: GREEN LITERACY PRACTICE CORRELATED WITH INTERNATIONAL BACCALAUREATE PRIMARY AND MIDDLE PLANNERS

If you are teaching in an International Baccalaureate (IB) curriculum, we show how we correlate Green Literacy Thematic Teaching Units with Primary and Middle Planners within the text of Green Heroes Series.

CHILDREN'S LITERATURE REFERENCES

Baker, J. (1988). *Where the forest meets the sea.* New York, NY: Greenwillow Books.

Bang, M. (1997). *Common ground: The water, earth, and air we share.* New York, NY: The Blue Sky Press

Breitrose, P. (2013). *Mousemobile.* New York, NY: Disney Hyperion Books.

Cherry, L. (2004). *The sea, the storm, and the mangrove tangle.* New York, NY: Farrar, Straus, & Giroux.

Facklam, M. (1993). *And then there was one: The mysteries of extinction.* New York, NY: Little, Brown.

Gall, C. (2013). *Awesome Dawson.* New York, NY: Little Brown.

Johnson, J. C. (2010). *Seeds of change*. New York, NY: Lee & Low Books.

Krouse Rosenthal, A., & Linchtenfield, T. (2009). *Duck! Rabbit!* San Francisco, CA: Chronicle Books.

Kamkwamba, W., & Mealer, B. *The boy who harnessed the wind: Creating currents of electricity and hope*. New York, NY: Harper Perennial.

McMillan, B. (2007). *How the ladies stopped the wind*. New York, NY: Houghton Mifflin.

O'Garden, I. (2013). *Forest, What would you like?* New York, NY: Holiday House.

Rawls, W. (1961). *Where the red fern grows*. New York, NY: Doubleday.

Rockwell, A. (2006). *Why are the ice caps melting? The dangers of global warming*. New York, NY: Harper Collins.

Rosenthal, A. K. (2009). *Duck! Rabbit!* San Francisco, CA: Chronicle Books.

Seuss, D. (1971). *The lorax*. New York, NY: Random House.

Silverstein, S. (1964). *The giving tree*. New York, NY: Harper & Row.

Tresselt, A. R. (1965). *Hide and seek fog*. New York, NY: Harper Collin**Green Heroes:**

K-5 Teaching Unit: How Do Young People Become Green Heroes/ Environmental Leaders?

● ● ●

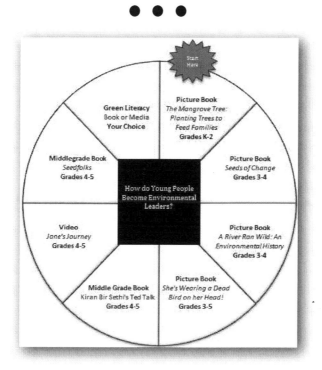

What's Inside:

- Grades K-2 Teaching Demonstration with further suggested other titles that could be used with the same teaching strategies.
- Grades 3-4 teaching activities with suggested other titles that could be used with the same teaching strategies.
- Suggested Grade 4-5 and Beyond teaching activities with suggested other titles that could be used with the same teaching strategies.
- Teaching strategies are highlighted and explained. The abbreviated letters/ numbers of the Common Core State Standards are provided in the charts within the Teaching Unit. You can find the unabbreviated Common Core State Standards for each teaching activity in Appendix B.

GREEN HEROES AND INTERNATIONAL BACCALAUREATE PRIMARY AND INTERMEDIATE PLANNERS

Joann is a 5th grade teacher at an urban school working to attain status as International Baccalaureate (IB) School. During the summer, Joann meets with her 5th grade teacher colleagues, Helen and Aisha, brainstorming how they want to teach How We Organize Ourselves, the IB "trans-disciplinary" unit. IB is a new school wide directive being implemented this school year.

Joann: I just bought *Green Heroes*. I read a review of it on Amazon and took a chance on ordering it. This could be a great model for us to use as we plan the How we Organize the Planet unit. Plus, there are commentaries. I have read part of Green Hero commentaries, they pushed my thinking, that's why I like it. What do you think Helen?

Helen: Last time we met we said we wanted to look at the concept of forms of leadership that influence conflict resolution and peace. I want to stick to developing that concept.

Joann: Bingo! That is why using *Green Heroes* as a model interests me. Look how the Green Literacy authors suggest using *Seedfolks*, a film about Jane Goodall and a TED lecture on an I Can School. The central concept is leadership.

Helen: Hum, let me take a look. I have used the book *Seedfolks* with my class at my old school and it worked well. My students really liked it. Any tie-in with multimedia and you've got my struggling readers interested.

Aisha: You know there is a big push to incorporate CCSS. We got to get that in there. Will this "model" as you call it, kind of hand hold me through the CCSS and not drag me down?

Joann, Helen, and Aisha meet a week later. Each has spent some time perusing *Green Heroes.*

Joann: So what do you think?

Aisha: Well one thing I think the ideas in *Green Heroes* will help me with is getting the kids into action. Last year, Ron, the IB consultant kept talking about this... I think the ideas in this book will help me get my kids to be more thoughtful and perhaps more likely they will come up with actions they initiate, not ones us teachers initiate --- remember that is what IB emphasizes.

Helen: What I liked was the commentary--- It made me think about community, awareness of our actions on others and our environments, strength in numbers, how we pass on traditions- to question what are we passing on. All of this is connected----I may have come up with all this on my own---- but who has time for that?

Aisha: I thought the way this Green Heroes made me think about teaching biography and leadership was out of the box thinking. I would like to use these lessons "as a model" as you said Joann. I will probably tweak some of these lessons though....

As the teachers in this vignette illustrate *Green Heroes* provides commentary and a model for teaching themes with an Inquiry question:

How do young people become Green Heroes /environmental leaders?

How Do Young People Become Green Heroes?
Commentary

Environmental issues are complex, multilayered, and need multiple perspectives in order to attain sustainable solutions. Many environmental challenges draw young people into hard dilemmas of determining solutions that may require sacrifices. Young people who become environmental leaders advocate visions that move environmental problems to possibilities.

Working with biographies in texts and digital media, we examine how individuals become environmental leaders. Within this Teaching Unit we examine the question: *How do young people become environmental leaders?* The books and digital media within these pages highlight different journeys of environmental leaders and their movements. In thinking about how to become environmental leaders, young people consider how events and people shape the lives of environmental leaders in selected books and digital media. These environmental leaders and their movements inspire and act as models for young people to become environmental leaders in their own communities.

All of the environmental leaders and the people in their movements in these texts and media share attributes of leadership and of environmental awareness. We believe as young people become environmental leaders they will: 1) acknowledge the earth and all living things are equal to human beings in the right to co-exist sustainably, 2) empower others through attitude shifts from problem to possibility thinking so that various resources are used to solve complex environmental challenges, and 3) work collaboratively and locally, often to influence global awareness.

Many young people involved in environmental issues participate because they believe that their contributed actions will help change degradation of the natural world. Many young people ask: *If I help and nothing changes, why should I care? If I work hard and come up with a viable solution and people in positions of power ignore my solution or belittle me, why should I try?* How do adults, people in power over young people, answer this question? What message can society instill in young people so that they can discover answers, push back and demand that the adult world pay attention to them? In many ways the question *Why should I try?* speaks to the reality that young people are not invited into the conversation.

Through storytelling and teaching, tellers explain that humans must work together in order to sustain individual motivation for a project. Consider the advent of the skyscraper, the development of the Internet, or the foundation of robotic surgery. These accomplishments cannot be attributed to one man or woman. Sure, the seed idea may belong to an individual, but collectively, many people contributed to each of these achievements, and in turn, more growth and movement evolved. We believe that young people may follow a leader but need to work as a group as environmental stewards.

In many cases, community takes the contributions of one individual and uses them to add value to the whole. The community supports the individual just as the individual supports the collective. On the surface, many assume there is a disconnection between the two. In fact, as young people push their perspective, the opposite proves true. Both rely on each other in order to function; if there is an absence of one, the other fails to thrive.

Environmental leaders, such as the ones highlighted in this Teaching Unit, began by acting locally. They started where they lived and discovered a problem in their local world. This problem ignited in them the willingness to speak up, and in doing so they became leaders. They received a wider audience and influenced people beyond their local community. In other words, the local situation helped create their environmental leadership.

Through time and effort, these environmental leaders brought to light a deep and complex danger happening in their local environment. Solutions to these dangers entailed people changing their opinions and actions. These environmental leaders have a vision that will cause change. Others do not want to change until a situation escalates and they are forced, or they recognize that the change would positively impact their lives. Another common thread between all the environmental leaders within this Teaching Unit is that each moves from the problem into the possibility. In other words, the environmental leaders are not stuck within conventional problem emphasis thinking; rather they vision and bring into reality a solution that benefits both community relationships and earth stewardship.

In this Teaching Unit, we focus on the biography. We chose biography because we want young people to recognize different types of environmental leadership and how these leadership styles connect to individuals and the movement.

GREEN LITERACY/ HEROES' APPROACH TO BIOGRAPHY

In reading and literature classes, teachers and students alike acknowledge the acts of one important individual person: the main character. Readers consider the fate of the protagonist, the journey of one person whose life radically changes due to his or her heroic act. In literary analysis we ask if the character's action is strong or weak? Does she overcome obstacles? Does her action help the whole?

In the conventional sense, biography invites young readers to "live" a hero's life.

Text and images support imagination. Armed with the ability to role-play and a keen sense of wonder, young people imagine themselves doing courageous actions, similar to the feats in the text and illustrations. More importantly, the study of biography magnifies and multiplies. With critical discussions, a biography can swell into the study of how one's life connects to others and how heroic feats become one of many strings that weave through a community story.

Consider then the traditional biography. Critics praise the pioneer spirit. The harder the job, the bigger the character becomes. The biography of one person may become symbolic for an entire community. Rachel Carson died fifty years ago after writing the best seller *Silent Spring* as well as other books. Her writing is credited with advancing the global environmental movement. Late in the 1950s Rachel Carson focused on synthetic pesticides. *Silent Spring* (1962) brought environmental concerns to an unprecedented share of American people. Even though the movement met fierce opposition by the chemical companies, it spurred a reversal in national pesticide policy, including a ban on DDT. Rachel Carson's work inspired a grassroots environmental movement that led to the creation of the US Environmental Protection Agency. Rachel Carson's story does not represent all environmentalists, yet most people recognize her as a symbol of the Environmental Movement. In her case and many others, the biography takes on mythic proportions that impact the community's shared story. A biography then is more than the narrative of one person's life and oftentimes represents the movement's story. The biography manifests into the story of movements and community as well as the individual. This is a delicate balance between an individual and the group or movement.

Green Literacy acknowledges that a biography expands from the inward journey of an individual outward to the community's story, particularly to those who support the leader. The genre when looked at though the lens of environmental leadership is more than the narrative of one person's life and oftentimes represents the story of the movement, community or even the natural resource. This is a delicate balance between an individual, the people in the movement or community and the natural resources that need to be conserved.

APPROACHES TO BIOGRAPHIES

* **Traditional Readers' Approach to Biography**: when readers concentrate on a written detailed description or account of a person's life emphasizing the person's actions.
* **Green Literacy's Readers' Approach to Biography**: when readers consider and give equal importance to all connections made in a person's life, especially those deep connections between projects and movements which shift the perspective from problem to possibility.

The Mangrove Tree: Planting Trees to Feed Families

COMMENTARY: BIOGRAPHY OF A PROJECT
The picture book, *The Mangrove Tree: Planting Trees to Feed Families* by Susan L. Roth and Cindy Trumbore is a powerful example of a community coming together to change environmental problems into an environmental possibility. Cell biologist Dr. Gordon Sato started a project growing mangrove trees by the shore of the salty Red Sea so that the

local herds of sheep and goats could eat the leaves as a new food source.

The subject matter of *The Mangrove Tree* makes it an important resource on sustainability. Behind the scenes of this book, years of conflict, economic stagnation, and famine devastated the people of the Eritrean village, Hargigo. They suffered from malnutrition and struggled with their well-being. They were stuck in "environmental problems" until an innovative idea of "environmental possibility" led to dramatic changes in the local food chain. Through Dr. Sato's influence, women who planted and tended the seedlings received training in fertilizing the young trees with special nutrients that would allow the trees to grow in salt water. Shepherds learned how to complement the mangrove leaves with seeds and fish so the herds would produce healthier milk. Local fishermen brought home larger catches because the mangrove roots served as homes for small sea creatures that attracted bigger fish.

Dr. Sato and the townspeople made changes by planting and fertilizing mangrove trees, which provided food for the herds of sheep and goats as well as firewood. Feeding the herds then provided food for the people of Hargigo, Eritrea.

The authors employ a motivating technique: On the left side of the page, the young person finds a "House That Jack Built"-type summary of the story as it unfolds. Most young readers know this step-by-step format. They recall how the story unfolds and predict what happens next. This format also helps young people keep track of what has happened in the previous part of the story. It cleverly illustrates how everything links together, from the planting of seedlings to the people who tend to them, so the seedlings may become the trees that provide sustenance for so many. The detailed description of the implementation of Dr. Sato's vision on the right side of the page entices more experienced readers. The text style, the message, and the collage illustrations engage and extend young readers' concept of storytelling.

GRADES K-2 THEMATIC TEACHING: ENVIRONMENTAL LEADERS

Suggested Text	Teaching Components Leading to In-depth Dialogue
The Mangrove Tree: Planting Trees to Feed Families by Susan L. Roth and Cindy Trumbore	Teacher reads aloud, with students' wonderings, questions, and thoughts about the author's ideas, writing, and illustrations.

Grade Level CCSS Standards: RI K.1, RI 1.1, RI 2.1, SL K, 1, 2SL K,.1, SL1.1, 2.1, SL K.2, 1.2, 2.2

Second Grade Vignette: Encouraging Young Environmental Leaders

Katie, a second grade Green Literacy teacher at an International Baccalaureate school in an urban area of Colorado, read *The Mangrove Tree: Planting Trees to Feed Families* to her class. She began the lesson with a map that displayed South America and Africa.

"Why do places far away from each other have things in common?" Katie asked.

One student replied, "They both have much heat." Katie told the class to keep "the heat" in mind.

After she read the book's title, she showed her students the cover. "What observations can you make about the cover?"

Jasmine said, "Maybe they have seeds to plant."

Katie said, "Yes, maybe so," and then posed, "What about their clothes?"

"Most of them dressed like the people in the rainforest," said Terrell.

"The man in the blue suit looks like our clothes," said Victor, and made a connection between the man's clothes and where his father works.

As Katie began reading the book, she wondered aloud, "How could a tree make families not hungry anymore?"

Students responded with different ideas, including "growing food" and "animals living in the trees." To these and others answers, Katie said, "Great ideas."

In a similar fashion, Katie guided her students with questions about the text as she read. Periodically, students made observations about the collages. Other students offered wonderings such as, "What do they use the tree trunk for?" Another student concluded, "Houses and boats." Students built a Text-to Text connection with another book about the rainforest in which animals made their homes in trees as they did in the mangrove trees.

Supportive of all observations, Katie encouraged connections, observations, and wonderings her students made throughout the book. On two occasions she asked, "What is your evidence? Why do you think so?" At another point a student made an observation that *The Mangrove Tree* occurred in the rainforest. Katie did not judge the answer as incorrect. Instead she asked the student if this book occurred in the rainforest and the student said, "Sort of." Katie moved on with reading the next page of the book. She would come back later to this student's confusion about Eritrea being in the rainforest.

After the discussion, students took out their Wonder Journals to write any questions that went through their minds as they listened to the story. She said, "Also, write about changes that happened in the village Hargigo because of the planting of the mangrove trees. Tomorrow we will get out our iPads and see if we find answers to our wonderings. Plus we will share changes that occurred to Hargigo because of the mangrove trees."

One girl said, "I don't have any Wonderings."

Katie said, "No wonders? Here, look at the book to help you." The girl got her journal, looked at the book, and began writing.

The next day, Katie and her students talked about their questions and the answers they found on the iPad. Then Katie asked the students, "Do you think after reading and talking about *The Mangrove Tree*, we need to write a new Green Literacy Ideal?"

Some students agreed. Others were not so sure.

"I think we can add something about food sources," Katie said. "What do we notice about the changes that happened in the Hargigo community once the mangrove trees grew?"

"The mangrove leaves were fed to the goats," said Lucy.

"Branches of the trees were used to build fires," offered Tyson.

"Because they had more goats they had more meat to eat," said Hunter.

"And more milk to drink," chimed in Alice.

Katie entered in, "What could we write as a Green Literacy Ideal?"

"You have to have new ideas to get better," said Nico.

"I agree with Nico. Class, what's the new idea Dr. Sato brought to Hargigo? Let's discuss." Katie said. After the discussion, the class created a Green Literacy Ideal building on Nico's contribution: *Often new ideas can be worked on and bring about many good things.* In this case the new idea was growing mangrove trees and the good things were more food and firewood.

This second grade example of *The Mangrove Tree* shows how Katie engaged with the K-2 age level where the children came up with their wonderings, questions, and thoughts about the author's ideas, writing, and illustrations. Using this open-ended, supportive dialogue, the class also developed a Green Literacy Ideal concerning the mindset needed for new ways of doing things that bring about new food sources.

OTHER SUGGESTED READINGS AND VIEWINGS

Here are some other picture books that could be used in K-2 classrooms that focus on the theme of developing leadership and initiating environmental projects. We suggest that you, as did Katie, follow the teaching strategies of having young people to come up with *their wonderings, questions, and thoughts about the author's ideas, writing, and illustrations.*

- Albert, Richard E. *Alejandro's Gift*. Sylvia Long, Illustrator. (1994). Chronicle Books: San Francisco. Lonely in his house beside a road in the desert, Alejandro builds an oasis to attract the many animals around him.
- *The True Blue Scouts of Sugar Man Swamp*. (2014). New York, NY: Atheneum Books for Young Readers. Raccoon brothers Bingo and J'miah are the newest recruits of the Official Sugar Man Swamp Scouts.

Grades 3-5 Recommendations

Thematic Teaching: Launching 3 Cycles of Comprehension

Focus	Suggested Texts/Media	Teaching Components Leading to In-depth Dialogue	Grade Level CCSS Standards
Biography of a River	*A River Ran Wild* by Lynn Cherry	**Simple Comprehension** *Listen to read aloud with free response writing * Write Dear Agony Letters to characters * Develop a timeline	CCSS RI 3.1 CCSS RI 4.1
		Criteria Comprehension *Provide reasons why this is a biography of a river * Write Dear Character letters from the river at the different time frames **Critical Perspective Taking** *Compare attitudes and actions of Chie Weeawa's people, the people during the Industrial Revolution, and Marion Stoddard and people who worked with her	CCSS RI 3.3 CCSS RI 4.3 CCSS RI 3.1 CCSS RI 3.7 CCSS RI 4.1 CCSS RI 4.7
			CCSS RL3.6 CCSS RL 4.2 CCSS RI 5.2 CCSS RI 3.7 CCSS RI 4.7

		Simple Comprehension	
Biography of a Movement	*Seeds of Change* by Jen Cullerton Johnson	**Simple Comprehension**	CCSS RI 3.1
		*Listen to read aloud with free response writing	CCSS RI 4.1
		Criteria Comprehension	
		*Provide reasons for connections in a Think Pair Share	
			CCSS RI 3.1
			CCSS RI 4.1
			CCSS RL 3.2
		Critical Perspective	CCSS RI 3.7
		*Drama Strategies:	CCSS RI 4.1
		Find voices and Enact to Solve and Issue	CCSS RI 4.7
		*Complete a Venn Diagram to compare *A River Ran Wild* and *Seeds of Change*	CCSS RL3.6
			CCSS RL 4.2
			CCSS RI 5.2
Biography of Activism	*She's Wearing a Dead Bird on Her Head* by Kathy Lasky	**Simple Comprehension**	CCSS RI 3.1
		*Listen to read aloud with free response writing	CCSS RI 4.1
			CCSS RI 4.7
		*Practice and perform two Readers Theatres	
		*Compare present time to that of Dickey Downey	
		Criteria Comprehension	CCSS RI 3.9
		*Consider what actions Minna and Harriet and Marion Stoddard took to change laws to student present day actions	CCSS RI 4.9
			CCSS RI 3.1
			CCSS RI 3.7
			CCSS RI 4.1
			CCSS RI 4.7

		Critical Perspective Comprehension *Compare the "preachy" factor of texts with environmental themes	CCSS RI 5.2 CCSS RI 5.3 CCSS RI.3.6 CCSS RL 4.2
Comparing themes	*A River Ran Wild* by Lynn Cherry * *Change* by Jen Cullerton Johnson * *She's Wearing a Dead Bird on Her Head* by Kathy Lasky	**Critical Perspective** **Comprehension** *Identify and compare themes *Support with details *Each student decide which of 3 themes she thinks in most important and why *Discuss importance of individual and groups' accomplishments	CCSS RI 3.9 CCSS RI 4.9 CCSS RI 5.9 CCSS RL 4.6 CCSS RL 4.9

Twelve-year-old Chap Brayburn is not a member, but he loves the swamp something fierce, and he'll do anything to help protect it. And help is needed, because world-class alligator wrestler Jaeger Stitch wants to turn the swamp into an Alligator World Wrestling Arena and Theme Park.

* Halsey, Megan. (2000). *3 Pandas Planting.* New York, NY: Aladdin Paperbacks. A colorful counting book combines information about nature with tips on preserving the environment, presenting such ideas as planting trees, carpooling, watching out for polluters, and enjoying the special gifts of the earth

A RIVER RAN WILD COMMENTARY: BIOGRAPHY OF RIVER

Unlike traditional biographies that require a human life to evaluate, readers have an opportunity to shift their perspective with Cherry's *A River Ran Wild*. Readers may take the viewpoint of the animals, the trees, the fishes, and the river. Many readers see the river as the protagonist and humans as the antagonists who pollute the river with toxic chemicals and sewage. Readers shift perspective from a person's point of view toward nature's point of view. Readers learn including living things must be part of the solution in restoring the earth's balance.

Lynn Cherry's book *A River Ran Wild* is a biography of the Nashua River and its parallel relationship with people who lived and worked along its shores. Like a botanist's field guide, the mosaic illustrations depict the changes in all the living things, such as red-tailed hawks, barred owls, geese, and deer. Young readers see how one species is prevalent in one era only to become extinct in another. The pictorial history of the river lends to the significance of the text, which offers insight into ecological change. Each environmental moment connects to a historical moment, and each shows the human impact on the health of the river. The story begins with the serene Native Americans who respected the river, moves forward to Colonial times when men claimed the river, and leads up to the industrial era when toxic chemicals from mills polluted the river *until* many decades later Marion Stoddard and a group of committed individuals cleaned up the river. The efforts of Stoddard and the Nashua Committee for Concerned Citizens helped pass the Clean Water Bill and restored the river back to its natural state.

Teaching Strategies for *A River Ran Wild*
Cycle 1: Simple Comprehension
Free Response Strategy
Writing Dear Agony Letters
Developing a Time Line

Cycle 2: Criteria Comprehension
Writing Dear Character Letters

Cycle 3: Critical Comprehension
Consider Attitudes and Actions toward Nashua River of different time periods

Cycle 1: Simple Comprehension *A River Ran Wild*
As teachers read *A River Ran Wild* in Free Response strategy, provide time and opportunity for young people to view and study the small framing pictures and the magnificent large artwork on each open page. As young people share their responses in small groups and as a class, they may

integrate aspects of the story they might have missed if read on their own.

To support students in further internalizing these stories, have them write Dear Agony Letters for each of the books. To write a Dear Agony Letter, a student chooses one character from the book and writes a letter to Dear Agony explaining what is wrong. Then another student responds back as Agony. This is a non-traditional way for students to grapple with what characters think and feel as well as what happens in the story. Each young person shares his or her letters with a small group or the class. This strategy reinforces Simple Comprehension or a mutual knowledge of what happens in each story.

Example of Dear Agony Letter
January 5, 1851

Dear Agony,

My name is Oweana and the river by where I live has gotten too polluted because of the paper mills. The paper is clogging up the river and it is making it smell. The paper changes the water to whatever color the paper was dyed in the mills. The fish can't live in the river. The birds have stopped making nests in the trees and the river is dying. Can you please give the Nashuas, my tribe, and me some advice on how to stop the problem? We need as much advice as you can give us.

Yours sincerely,

Oweana

Example of Response Letter

February 1, 1851

Dear Oweana,

I am sorry to hear about your problem, and I have a few ideas on what you can do to fix it. You can start talking to people in your community and see if you can get someone to talk to the people who run the paper mills. Another idea is to protest against the paper mills and not buy paper from them. Remember, though, do not do anything that can cause any harm to anyone or you and your tribe could get in trouble. Another idea is to send letters to the government and ask them for help. Another idea is for you and your tribe to work to clean up the river. By doing this, you may show the paper company that you care deeply and they may have a change of heart and fix the problem.

Best to you,

Agony

Developing a Timeline

A final way to hone into Simple Comprehension for *A River Runs Wild* is to pair students to devise a timeline of what happens to the Nashua River over pre-industrial to present day. Have students study the pictures/images in the book to create their timeline. In the timeline, encourage them to describe the image, the event, and the impact of the event on the Nashua River. Then ask students to consider how present types of pollution may impact the Nashua River and what may need to be done in the future so that the Nashua River continues to "run wild."

Timeline for *A River Ran Wild*, 1400 – 2012

Directions: Using the images in *A River Ran Wild*, create a timeline for the biography of the Nashua River. Focus on how each event portrayed in the images impacted the next event.

Cycle 2: Criteria Comprehension *A River Ran Wild*

Bring to the class the idea that this is a biography of the Nashua River watershed. Students give reasons why this seems accurate to them or not. Have them support their reasons with information from the text. For example, the young people may say, "Yes I think it is a biography of the Nashua River because it tells the life of the river from when Indians lived there to when it was polluted with mills and finally cleaned up. So it tells the life of the river."

Next, young people choose a time frame from their timeline of the Nashua River, then write a Dear Character letter from the river as a character in the story at that point in time to the people in the timeframe chosen.

Student Example of Dear Character letter from Nashua River to Marion
May 17, 1968

Dear Marion,

Thank you so much for working to restore me to health. I hated being so smelly and polluted. Plus all the fish that used to swim in me had died and I missed them. I know you did a lot of work to get this done. You traveled to all the towns along the river. You got people to sign petitions. You protested to politicians. You convinced the paper mills to process their waste instead of dumping it into me. Plus, new laws were passed so that the factories stopped polluting me.

I am so happy that now I flow cleanly, freely, happily. And people enjoy being in and around me.

Thanks again, forever grateful,

Nashua River

Cycle 3: Critical Perspective Comprehension
A River Ran Wild

To develop Critical Comprehension, involve the young people in this suggested learning activity:

(1) In small groups, young people complete the chart, comparing the attitudes and actions toward the

river by Chief Weeawa's people, the people during the Industrial Revolution, and Marion Stoddard and the people who worked with her.

ATTITUDES & ACTIONS TOWARD NASHUA RIVER

(2) Students explore connections to their own lives and contemplate which of these three kinds of attitudes and behaviors of the characters most resemble their own ideas and why.

(3) "Push" students to dig deeply into their own personal experiences so that they make connections by having them cite evidence from the text.

(4) Inquire: What kind of attitudes, thinking, and actions do we need in the future to continue to keep the river clean? Why do you think so?

Continue to pose higher level thinking questions until students successfully form individual opinions. Students write their opinions and provide support from the text about why they think this way.

SEEDS OF CHANGE, COMMENTARY, BIOGRAPHY OF A MOVEMENT
The picture book, *Seeds of Change* by Jen Cullerton Johnson exemplifies a biography of both a person and a movement. One

storyline centers on the leader and the catalyst of the movement. The other parallel storyline focuses on the movement and the people who supported and shared the leader's vision. Both perspectives blend together, creating a whole story.

Seeds of Change tells the life story of Wangari Maathai, who became the first African woman, and environmentalist, to win a Nobel Peace Prize. She blazed a trail across Kenya, using her knowledge and compassion to promote the rights of her countrywomen and help save the land, one tree at a time, through the Green Belt Movement. In many ways Wangari's life story mirrors the Green Belt Movement, an organization she founded. Wangari's vision became a mutual mission with others in the Green Belt Movement. The Green Belt's message was simple: work together and results will come.

Students take the Green Belt's message one step further and interpret its meaning as evidence that when people work together, collective results have a domino effect, inviting others' participation. When students evaluate Wangari's life and the lives of those within the Green Belt Movement, they realize that biography is more than one person's life and is rather many lives woven together; they move from the problem of deforestation and poverty to the possibility of financial independence and rebuilding an ecosystem.

TEACHING STRATEGIES FOR *SEEDS OF CHANGE*
CYCLE 1: SIMPLE COMPREHENSION
Free Response Strategy

CYCLE 2: CRITERIA COMPREHENSION
Think Pair Share

CYCLE 3: CRITICAL COMPREHENSION
Engagement Strategy: Step 1- Finding the Voices; Step 2- Enacting to Solve an Issue

CYCLE 1: SIMPLE COMPREHENSION *SEEDS OF CHANGE*

During Simple Comprehension, the class arrives at a mutual understanding about what took place in the story and in the life of the main character and those people who helped her vision. To do this, the Green Literacy teacher uses the Free Response Strategy as she reads each book aloud. Free Response Strategy is when the teacher stops at pre-selected spots within the story and asks comprehension questions.

In order to implement Free Response, the teacher reads the book alone and decides on four or five places to stop so that when she reads the story aloud, the young people may write their comments and share them with the class. The Free Response Strategy gives students time for response through comments in writing /discussing the story, plot, or characters which reveal their perceptions and preoccupations about the story. All responses ring correctly as long as the responses relate to the text in some way.

CYCLE 2: CRITERIA COMPREHENSION *SEEDS OF CHANGE*

In this learning activity young people make personal connections to *Seeds of Change* using the Think Pair Share. Think Pair Share (Lyman, 1981) is a useful engagement tool for all students; even the shyest student will be involved.

THINK PAIR SHARE

Think: Start with a question/prompt that gets the students thinking about the story. Students are given a short amount of time to reflect on the question.

Pair: Students pair up with a partner and share their responses. The goal is for the partners to compare their information and come up with the most complete response to the question.

Share: Each pair shares their responses with the whole class.

Students explain why their connection is pertinent. For example, suppose after reading about the protagonist Wangari Maathai, one student says his connection is that he saw a bulldozer take down a grove of trees for a condominium development in his neighborhood. The student then elaborates on how this is connected to Wangari's life.

Come back together in larger group at the end of the Think Pair Share and continue the discussion using the following questions:

* What did Wangari do when she saw that trees had been cut down in Kenya?
* What happened with the people who supported Wangari's vision?
* What evidence is there about the importance of how community supports the individual? Students cite evidence in the text.
* Focus on the reasons, rationale, and criteria students provide. Emphasize these in the discussion, especially where students differ. For example, a student could say the condo is needed so more people could live in the neighborhood. Another may say, but green space is needed for play and provides oxygen to decrease greenhouse gasses.

CYCLE 3: CRITICAL PERSPECTIVE COMPREHENSION
SEEDS OF CHANGE

Lead the young people into an Engagement Strategy (Long & Gove, 2004), a dramatic two-step strategy that promotes critical thinking concerning what differing characters think and feel.

Step One: Finding the Voices. In this example, we choose four voices or "points of view": the Green Belt women who listen to Wangari and plant 30 million trees in Kenya; Wangari's friends at the university in Kenya; the wealthy businessmen who pay corrupt police officers to arrest Wangari; and Wangari, herself, freed from jail. The class forms four groups. Each group brainstorms about what these people think and say. Then the groups share their ideas with the class as a whole.

Step Two: Enacting to Solve an Issue. The class then re-enacts the trial of Wangari. The students act out Wangari herself, her Kenyan university friends, the Green Belt women who worked with her to plant trees, and the wealthy businessmen who worked with police to put Wangari behind bars. The teacher plays the part of the judge. She asks the class to make their case, drawing from the ideas developed in Step One. To stage this enactment, the teacher explains what is occurring and then turns around. When the teacher faces the class again, she is the judge. Class participants present to the judge their beliefs about why Wangari should or should not be freed. The judge may then rule that Wangari should be freed or that some other action is necessary. Upon the conclusion of the enactment, one person plays Wangari and describes what she plans to do next and why. Through this process, young people think deeply about the issues surrounding Wangari's imprisonment and her feelings and ideas concerning what she may decide to do after her sentence.

SHE'S WEARING A DEAD BIRD ON HER HEAD!
COMMENTARY: BIOGRAPHY OF ACTIVISM

Although *She's Wearing A Dead Bird on Her Head* is a fictional account based on historical facts, we consider the lives of Harriet and Mina and their interaction with women's rights and the foundation of the Audubon Society to be a biography of activism. This book portrays two real life women's political activism that helped pass laws to protect birds in the early 1900s. Their activism was tied to the conservation movement. Historical figures Harriet Hemenway and her cousin Minna Hall raised awareness about several species of birds that were becoming extinct because of their use in women's fashion. Fashion was indirectly linked to women's rights, and during the Victoria era women did not have the right to vote.

Women at the turn of the century came together to lobby for equality as well as for preservation of birds. They realized that a woman who wore a dead animal on her head for the sake of fashion would not be taken seriously and that women needed to reconsider this fashion trend. They worked with other women and men to pass laws that prevented the killing of birds for fashion, and then pushed for the laws to be enforced. Women and men with persistence and commitment in a similar movement worked together to usher in the 19th Amendment, which secured the right to vote for women.

Young people can learn the basic steps to become environmentally active. Through this story they identify *how* to have a voice in the public arena even though the public devalued women's status. Since young people do not have the right to vote, similar to Harriet and Minna, they can start letter writing campaigns and influence government officials by gathering information so that laws can be written and enforced.

TEACHING STRATEGIES FOR *SHE'S WEARING A DEAD BIRD ON HER HEAD!*
CYCLE 1 SIMPLE COMPREHENSION
Experimenting with voices and Readers' Theatre Analyzing Actions of Harriet, Minna, Harriet's Husband, and Their Friends that were part of a movement that changed laws

CYCLE 2 CRITERIA COMPREHENSION
Small group to whole group discussion: the relationship of legislation to stop using birds for fashion to women acquiring the vote Comparing *She's Wearing a Dead Bird on her Head!* (1992) to *Dickey Downy (1903)*

CYCLE 3 CRITICAL COMPREHENSION
Rating books with an environmental theme for the "preachiness factor"

Cycle 1 Simple Comprehension *She's Wearing a Dead Bird on Her Head!*

During reading aloud, both the teacher and the young people can experiment with how the pinched-faced, proper, conservation-minded Harriet Hemenway and her cousin Minna Hall sounded when they spoke. Students can experiment with the voices of the women who wore dead birds on their hats and with Harriet's husband's voice. Afterwards, practice and then present a Reader's Theater, which was devised from the beginning of the book.

Readers' Theater of *She's Wearing a Dead Bird on Her Head!*

NARRATOR: Harriet is a very proper Boston lady – she never talked with her mouth full. But one day she almost did. Standing by a bay window in her parlor, she had just bitten into a jam cookie when her eyes sprang wide open in dismay. She gasped, leaned forward, swallowed, and then turned to her parlor maid.

HARRIET: She is wearing a dead bird on her head!

NARRATOR: Feathers on ladies' hats were becoming more and more popular. At first, hats had been decorated with just feathers, and then designers began to add pairs of wings. But this woman had an entire bird perched atop her hat! Harriet squinted her eyes as the lady of fashion walked proudly by.

HARRIET: Arctic tern.

PARLOR MAID: Looks ready to fly away.

HARRIET (sadly): It won't.

NARRATOR: Harriet felt that she had to do something. Huge populations of birds, from egrets to pheasants to owls to warblers, were being slaughtered for hat decoration – none was spared.

HARRIET: What can I do? Women have very little power. I can't vote. At least my husband does not treat me as many do. I can read the newspaper; I have friends whose husbands don't allow this.

NARRATOR: Harriet wanted to change things for ALL women. And she wanted to do something for the birds. Fashion was killing birds as well as killing women's chances to have the right to vote and be listened to. For who would listen to a woman with a dead bird on her head? And if senseless slaughter for a silly fashion were not stopped, in a few years the birds with the prettiest feathers would all be dead, gone forever, extinct.

HARRIET: I will call Cousin Minna.

NARRATOR: Minna was walking to tea with Harriet, and she saw in front of her a woman wearing a hat with a swirl of snowy egret feathers pinned to its crown.

MINNA: Revolting!

FASHIONABLE LADY WITH THE EGRET FEA-THERS ON HER HAT: Me?!

MINNA: You, you heartless creature! That bird should not be slaughtered just to make you feel pretty. Yeccch!

NARRATOR: When Minna stormed into the parlor, Harriet was preparing tea.

MINNA: Well Harriet, from Arlington Street to Clarendon—three egrets, one marabou, two grebes, one golden finch, and . . . a hummingbird!

HARRIET: Oh no, Minna!

MINNA: Oh yes, Harriet— perched in full flight on a bunch of silk roses with a veil.

HARRIET: Disgusting!

MINNA: Revolting!

HARRIET: Nauseating!

MINNA: Vile!

MINNA: Well, let's get down to business. Do you have the *Boston Social Register?* So we can write to all the grandest families in Boston.

She's Wearing A Dead Bird on Her Head! portrays two real life women's political activism that helped pass laws to protect birds in the early 1900s. We suggest Green Literacy teachers have students analyze Harriet and Minna's actions that were part of a movement that changed laws. So, have young people list the actions that Harriet, Minna, Harriet's husband, and their friends took in order to help save the different kinds of birds from extinction. The first two steps are already included. In brief, the women formed a club to protect the birds, persuaded men who could vote to join the club, worked to get laws enacted, and finally took action so that the laws were enforced. This is a model for movements that have made a difference in the lives of humans as well as in protecting the environment.

ACTIONS OF HARRIET, MINNA, HARRIET'S HUSBAND, AND THEIR FRIENDS
Some examples are provided.

1. Using the Boston Social Register, they wrote the names of fashionable ladies in Boston.
2. Decided to form a bird club to protect the birds.

After students complete list of actions discuss in whole group the following questions:

1. What did Harriet and Minna say about how women wearing birds on their heads would affect women getting the right to vote? Do you agree with this or not? Why or why not?
2. Since Harriet and Minna included men in their bird club, what happened when the men disagreed with the women? Cite from the text.
3. Do you think that the kinds of actions that Harriet and Minna did to save the birds could also be used to obtain women's right to vote? Why or why not?

These discussions will develop Simple Comprehension, an understanding of the plot and characters in the picture book.

COMPARING *SHE'S WEARING A DEAD BIRD ON HER HEAD!* TO *DICKEY DOWNY*

To further build background knowledge of the movement of saving the birds from the fashion world, have students read and perform another Readers' Theatre drawn from *Dickey Downy: An Autobiography of a Bird* by Virginia Sharpe Patterson, published in 1903. Patterson wrote *Dickey Downy* to support the early Audubon Society's campaign to end killing of birds for women's fashion. Patterson's efforts in environmental activism gave young readers the opportunity to consider a bird's point of view. Although fiction, readers contemplate the connections and disconnections between humans and the animal world. Comparing the ideas in the modern text *She's Wearing a Dead Bird on Her Head!* to *Dickey Downy*, written in 1903, is a valuable way to engage young people into the CCSS of comparing and integrating information from several texts on the same topic in order to write or speak about the subject knowledgeably. In this case young people consider texts on the topic of killing birds for fashion, one written near the turn of the century and one written in 1995.

Readers' Theater **from pages 33-40** *of Dickey Downy: An Autobiography of a Bird Dickey Downy: An*

Autobiography of a Bird by Virginia Sharpe Patterson was published in 1903. Patterson wrote it to promote the early Audubon Society's campaign to encourage the end of killing of birds to place them on women's hats – the subject of *She's Wearing A Dead Bird on Her Head* by Katherine Lasky. We have developed a Readers' Theatre from a portion of this book, which is in the Public Domain. Readers can find the entire book on our website, GreenLiteracy.org.

DICKEY DOWNY: My mother had hidden me, perched in a tree. Below me was a favorite spot of Miss Katie and her friends in her backyard. My mother had bidden me to look at them. And what did I see? I saw ladies' hats trimmed with dead birds. Fastened on sidewise, head downward, on one was a magnificent scarlet tanager, his body half concealed in the folds of tulle, his fixed eye staring into vacancy. On another was the head and breast of a beautiful yellowhammer; the tall sweeping plumes of the egret, which the bird produces only at breeding time, surrounded it. Oh, how much joy and beauty the world had lost by that cruel deed! How my heart sickened as I gazed at these pleasant, refined women flaunting the trophies of their cruelty in the beautiful sunlight.

Had they no compassion for the feathered mother who had been robbed of her young for the sake of a hat? Oh, how can they do such dreadful, such wicked things?

MOTHER: You see now who are our worst enemies. The cat preys on us to satisfy his bodily hunger, but women have no such excuse. We are not slaughtered to sustain lives but to minister to their vanity. For years, women have waged their unholy war against us. We have been driven from our haunts and forced to seek new places. Thousands have shot us every season so that now many species are destroyed from the face of the earth. The hunter hovers over the nest of her helpless offspring with as little compunction as if she were a poisonous reptile instead of the joy-giver. And all this horrible slaughter is for women.

DICKEY DOWNY: But why are they so cruel? Why do this wicked thing?

MOTHER: For the sake of Fashion.

DICKEY DOWNY: Fashion, what is that?

MOTHER: Well, Fashion is an exacting ruler, a great, tyrannical god who has many, many worshipers, and these he rules with an iron hand. His followers cannot be induced to do anything contrary to his wishes. He sits on a high throne from which he dictates to his slaves what they must do. Often they do the most outrageous things, not because they like to, but because he demands it. He is constantly laying down new laws for their guidance, and some of these laws are so unreasonable and absurd that a part of his followers frequently threaten to rebel. They do not hold out against him long, for he manages to make it quite unpleasant for those who disobey him or refuse to come under his yoke.

DICKEY DOWNY: Has he any men slaves?

MOTHER: Yes, he has some slaves among men, but the larger numbers of those who wear his most galling fetters are women. If he but crooks his little finger these bond-women rush pell-mell in the direction he points. They are thus keen to do his bidding, because each woman who is the first to carry out his rules in her own particular town or neighborhood acquires great distinction in the eyes of other worshipers.

DICKEY DOWNY: His slaves are nearly always rich women, aren't they?

MOTHER: By no means. Many of them are poor working women who have to labor for a living. Often it takes them a long time to follow his demands. Often just as they have accomplished the weary task, he suddenly proclaims a new law, and the toiling begins over again. Their chains are never lifted or lightened a particle.

DICKEY DOWNY: If the chain is so heavy, why don't they break it?

MOTHER: Because they are afraid.

DICKEY DOWNY: Afraid of the god?

MOTHER: No, no child, they are afraid of each other. They are afraid the richer slaves who are able to comply with the demands will laugh at them and ridicule them and that is why they strain every nerve to follow the god's wishes. A slave, whether she is rich or poor, grows more cringing year by year, until at last she loses all her individuality and becomes a mere echo of the god.

DICKEY DOWNY: What about the woman who is independent and won't worship the god?

MOTHER: Why, they call that kind of woman a crank – whatever that is.

DICKEY DOWNY: This Fashion is a cruel tyrant and that is why we are being killed!

CYCLE 2: CRITERIA COMPREHENSION *SHE'S WEARING A DEAD BIRD ON HER HEAD!*

Step 1: Have young people discuss their responses to these questions in small groups so that all will have a chance to engage their minds and share their thoughts.

- How were Harriet and Minna successful in their political action to get women to stop wearing dead birds on their hats even though they did not have the right to vote? Explain why you think so.
- How was Harriet and Minna's campaign related to women's suffrage? Why do you think so?

Emphasize the importance of writing reasons, rationale, and criteria for students' ideas as well as the importance of talking about them in small and whole groups.

Step 2: Move to a whole group discussion, making sure that each group shares their responses as well as supports their ideas by citing evidence from the text. Focus on the differing reasons or points of view that are brought forth in the discussion. For example, to the question, "How did Minna and Harriet stop women from wearing dead birds on their hats even though they did not have the right to vote?" a student may respond, "They got men like their husbands to help them." Why did that help? "Because men did have the right to vote." or "Many people like birds and didn't want them to become extinct." Why did that help? "So people would listen to the women because they spoke the truth." or "Women talk to each other and tell each other not to follow this fashion."

Step 3: Begin a dialogue where students connect the personal and the political. Probe them to discover if they know of something from their personal life that has become a political issue. Share with the young people that an issue is political when a group organizes to change laws as Marion Stoddard and Minna and Harriet did. Such efforts often meet with opposition from people who disagree with them.

CYCLE 3 CRITICAL PERSPECTIVE COMPREHENSION FOR *SHE'S WEARING A DEAD BIRD ON HER HEAD!*

A book reviewer from School Library claimed, "Lasky's title will entertain young readers while offering them a fascinating and little-known slice of history" (Engelfried, 1995). We agree. However, this book brings to mind when people care a lot about something that is, are passionate about something, such as the killing of birds for fashion, they may be called preachy or heavy-handed. We consider a text "preachy" when it feels like a lecture. Many environmental leaders are labeled as preachy. They often draw attention to grave environmental crises, such as global warming. In reality environmental leaders want people to understand the complex issues and encourage the pubic to take important action. Being "preachy" may occur when a writer takes a critical stance and wants readers to understand an issue. Frequently, being preachy occurs when people have not expanded their vision. For example, an environmentalist may constantly tell people, "Turn off the lights," which can be irritating, when the people involved do not understand that turning off lights conserves energy.

A reviewer of *She's Wearing a Dead Bird on Her Head!* felt the book was "preachy." The reason this critic gave was the author had Minna and Harriet put down the women who wore dead birds on their heads by calling what they were doing "*silly, disgusting, revolting, nauseating, and ghastly*" (Amazon, 2002).

Begin a critical dialogue using the following questions as a guide:

* Do you agree or disagree that this book is preachy? Why or why not?
* Would you think this is still a good book if Minna and Harriet put down the behavior of the women who wore birds on their heads? Why or why not?

- What do you think makes a book preachy?
- Why are people turned off by preachy books?

From this conversation begin to develop Critical Perspective Comprehension by having the class rate the "preachy" factor of the following texts (1) *She's Wearing a Dead Bird on Her Head!*, (2) the Readers' Theater version of *Dickey Downy: An Autobiography of a Bird*, and (3) an environmental picture book of student's choosing. Deciding whether or not a book may be too preachy is a complex task. Readers need to question what they are learning and how the author tells it. What do readers infer in terms of information and facts? Also, with how much of the writer's critical stance does the reader agree?

Next, use a scale of 1-5 to rate these books.

Preachy Factor

1 = Informative, interesting and not preachy at all.
2 = A little preachy, but I don't really notice it.
3 = Somewhat preachy, only bothers me a bit.
4 = Fairly preachy and rude to me.
5 = Really gets on my nerves, preaching or lecturing me – seems rude to me.

Students discuss within peer groups why they rate each book as they do. Then students support their ideas with evidence from the text. As before, students will have different opinions and that is OK.

After rating environmental books chosen by the students, lead students in developing Green Literacy Ideals concerning messaging about environmental issues. Students debate if it is important for our messaging not to be heavy-handed or preachy. If not, how can we do this and still get across how vital the environmental matter is?

COMMENTARY ABOUT LEADERS WORKING IN COMMUNITY TO EFFECT CHANGE
A River Ran Wild, Seeds of Change, and *She's Wearing a Dead Bird on Her Head!*

Consider Marion Stoddard and what happened to the Nashua River, and Wangari Maathai and what happened to Kenya's forests. Also, reflect on what happened to the fashion of women wearing dead birds on their hats at the turn of the 20th century. These women did not just simply *do*; their actions connected them to others. Wangari Maathai, Marion Stoddard, Harriet Hemenway, and Minna Hall valued strong connections between nature and human existence. The women solved problems creatively and collectively. They understood too that if a community could come together, there would be more success. They formed organizations such as the Green Belt Movement, the Nashua River Watershed Association, and the Audubon Society. A committed group of individuals protested and worked together, and after years of hard work, trees flourished in Kenya, the Nashua River sustained healthy aquatic life, and women no longer wore dead birds on their heads.

In many ways these women were environmental pioneers in socio-ecological problem solving that created possibilities from problems. They all had the ability to consider devastating and complex problems in their society. They evaluated how humans interact in their social environment and with nature. All of the women understood humanity's interconnections with the planet. Most importantly, their actions were not carried out alone.

Wangari Maathai, Marion Stoddard, Harriet Hemenway, and Minna Hall started where they were in the simplest location: where they lived. Instead of working on a problem far from home, their vision focused on what lay before them: the local ecology. They acted on what was before them. Their message of starting *where you are* is profound and deliberate.

Comparing Texts: *A River Ran Wild, Seeds of Change, and She's Wearing a Dead Bird on Her Head!*

In practice, Green Literacy students talk about how *Seeds of Change*, *A River Ran Wild*, and *She's Wearing a Dead Bird on Her Head!* are similar and/or different. After discussing ways these texts are similar, the Green Literacy teacher guides students in a discussion about what they think is the essential message of each author. Then, using the following information, each young person decides which of the three messages he/she thinks is the most important.

RECOGNIZING CENTRAL THEMES

We recognize there are several themes within each of the books, and student answers will vary. We provide central themes as a reference point for Green Literacy teachers.

> *A River Ran Wild*: Through laws and people putting effort into clean-up, natural resources regenerate.
> *Seeds of Change*: A small group of people work together for the common purpose.
> *She's Wearing a Dead Bird on Her Head!*: Through action to raise awareness such as writing letters and giving opinions to legislators, people make changes that help living beings.

Using the diagram below, have students consider traditional biography and how they may have shifted their thinking when they read these books. Engage students in dialogue around how the group story informs the individual story and vice-versa.

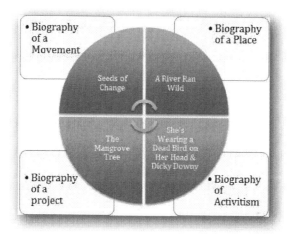

This discussion will likely bring into play many of the ideas mentioned in the beginning of this Teaching Unit:

* How important are one individual's accomplishments? Why?
* How important are a group's accomplishments? Why?
* How does one individual's accomplishments compare to a groups' accomplishments and vice-versa? Why?
* Which accomplishments may have a deeper/lesser impact on society? Why?

Once the discussion reaches conclusion, ask students if there are any Green Literacy Ideals that can be formed. Focus on the above questions to jumpstart dialogue and help create a classroom Green Literacy Ideal.

Here are some other picture books that could be used in 3-5 classrooms that focus on the theme of developing leadership and initiating environmental projects. We suggest that you use the teaching strategies described above with the following books:

BIOGRAPHY OF A PLACE:
Letting Swift River Go. New York, NY: Little, Brown and Company.

A young girl growing up in the safety and comfort of Swift River Valley watches as her town is flooded to supply water for the city of Boston.

BIOGRAPHY OF A MOVEMENT:
Rachel Carson: Preserving a Sense of Wonder. Golden, CO: Fulcrum Publishing.

From a small town in Pennsylvania came a little girl who saw the magic in spring fog and heard the ocean's song in her heart. In this engaging biography, young readers will experience the enchantment of nature as seen through the eyes of the budding naturalist.

BIOGRAPHY OF A PROJECT:
Belonging. London, UK: Walker Children's Paperbacks.

This is an account of the reclamation of an urban landscape told wordlessly through fascinating, detailed collage artwork.

Biography of Activism:
Michael Recycle Meets Litterbug Doug. San Diego, CA: Worthwhile Books.

Litterbug Doug hates recycling! The town where he lives is suffering from the stench released by the garbage that Doug leaves wherever he goes! It's up to Michael Recycle, planet Earth's green-caped to help. In the back there are two pages of trash facts from Doug, which are based on information from the U. S. Environmental Protection Agency, and two more of Go Green Tips from Michael himself. *Michael Recycle Meets Litterbug Doug* is printed on recycled paper.

Launching 3 Cycles of Comprehension with Longer, Complex Readings and Viewings

Grades 4, 5, and Beyond Recommendations

Focus	Suggested Texts/Media	Teaching Components Leading to In-depth Dialogue	Grade Level CCSS Standards
Biography of a Project	*Seedfolks* by Paul Fleishman	Simple & Criteria Comprehension	CCSS RI 4.1
		*Consider cover and make predictions	CCSS RI 4.6
		*Complete chart and discuss experiences of the voice in each Teaching Unit of *Seedfolks* and come up with "leadership actions" of characters	CCSS RL 5.1
			CCSS RI 4.7
			CCSS RI 5.2
			CCSS RL 4.2
			CCSS SL 5.1
			CCSS RI 5.2
			CCSS RI 4.2
			CCSS RL 5.1
		Critical Perspective Comprehension	CCSS SL 5.1
		*Participate in a Discussion Web concerning Do you think your neighborhood could use a catalyst (as the garden was in *Seedfolks*) to bring folks together?	CCSS RI 3.6
			RI 4.7
			RL 4.6

| Biography of a Human & Primate Friendship | *Jane's Journey* By Lorenz Knauer (video) | **Simple and Criteria Comprehension** *Describe what Jane does, who supported her in different times in her life *Describe Roots & Shoots projects described in film **Critical Perspective Comprehension** *Free write connections to *Jane's Journey* | CCSS RI 4.1 CCSS RI 5.2 |
| Biography of Kid Empowered Movement | *Kiran Bir Sethi's TED Talk* | **Simple & Criteria Comprehension** *Describe the "I Can" bug *Describe kid projects in the film * Involve in I Can!/ We Can! 6 Step Process *Free Write on projects students would like to pursue **Criteria & Critical Perspective Comprehension** *One idea, one week: 3 step process figuring out a project students would like to do | CCSS RI 4.1 CCSS RI 4.2 CCSS RI 4.7 CCSS RI 5.2 CCSS RI 5.1 CCSS RI 5.2 CCSS SL 5.1 |

COMMENTARY, BIOGRAPHY OF A PROJECT, *SEEDFOLKS*

We call *Seedfolks* a biography of a project because it shows many points of view about creating a community garden through different character voices. Although *Seedfolks* is realistic fiction, the way the stories are portrayed by the different characters underscores our concept that individual stories are connected to a larger community story.

Seedsfolks is a novel that focuses on multi-cultural urban life and how people hold on to stereotypes of others who are different from them. It is set in an economically challenged, diverse urban neighborhood in Cleveland where neighbors have little trust in each other, especially in those different from themselves. The novel begins with a young Vietnamese-American girl planting lima beans to honor her dead father in a neglected trash-filled lot. From this small start, a community garden project transforms the neighborhood to one where people help each other.

The story demonstrates how working together on a project can change point of view. A different member of the community tells each Teaching Unit in the first person. The reader considers that individual voices are heard, but conceptualized against the backdrop of the whole. Not all of the voices tell "rosy" stories; some, especially at the beginning of the book, are bleak. However, each story weaves together to build a community of voices. These voices are male and female from many age groups and ethnic backgrounds. By the end of the book, readers have heard a great diversity of voices developing or observing a neighborhood garden.

TEACHING STRATEGIES FOR *SEEDFOLKS*
Cycles 1 and 2 Simple Comprehension and Criteria Comprehension, Seedfolks
Pre-reading strategy considering the cover and make predictions of why the book is named *Seedfolks*.

During reading strategy, students write their thoughts on post-it notes.

Post reading strategy: consider the name of the book the author used and propose others, supporting ideas with items from their post-it notes.

Extended activity: Identify each character and how working in the garden with the other community members affected them. Also how each character took leadership actions.

CYCLE 3 CRITICAL PERSPECTIVE COMPREHENSION, *SEEDFOLKS*

Discussion Web Teaching Strategy: Do you think your neighborhood could use a catalyst to bring folks together?

Cycles 1 and 2 Simple Comprehension and Criteria Comprehension, Seedfolks

Part I: Pre Reading: As a pre-reading exercise, students think and write their responses to the following on a Post-it note:

1. Consider the front cover of the book with its many faces. What do these faces represent? What can you predict about the story from looking at the cover?

2. Why is the book titled *Seedfolks*? What words or images come to mind when thinking about the title and the front cover?

Part II: During Reading: While they read the book, have students write their thoughts on Post- it notes and keep them for reference. This way students will begin to organize their thoughts and be able to cite evidence in the text quickly when required..

Part III: Post Reading: Once students finish the book, as a post-reading discussion exercise,

1. Students discuss what the author says about the title (see pages 65-66.).
2. Students determine another name for the book and their reasons. Using their Post-it notes they created while reading the book, have them cite evidence
3. After the discussion of the Character Chart (See below), perhaps the next day, students talk through how each character took leadership actions. For example, a student may deem Leona 's initiative to travel to the Public Health Department to request the city to clean up the trash an act of leadership. As the class lists characters' leadership actions, have them cite from the text. As an example we completed the information for Kim, the first voice in Teaching Unit 1.
4. After the discussion of the Character Chart, perhaps the next day, talk through if young people think each character took leadership actions. For example, a student may deem Leona 's initiative to travel to the Public Health Department to request

the city to clean up the trash an act of leadership. As the class lists characters' leadership actions, have them cite from the text.

Person's Name	Country From	What drew him/her to the garden?	Draw a picture if you like.	Comment on her view of people different from her before working in the garden. Give reason why you think so.	Comment on her view of people different from her after working in the garden. Give reason why you think so.
Kim	Vietnam	To honor her dead father who had been a farmer in Vietnam.		Kim was frightened of people in neighborhood because when she found Wendell (who was white) watering her beans, she didn't say anything, only "her eyes got even bigger."	Not sure . . . but in the last Teaching Unit Florence told about a little Oriental girl planting beans early the next Spring.
Ana					
Wendell					
Gonzalo					
Leona					
Sam					
Virgil					
Nora					

Character Chart for *Seedfolks* by Paul Fleischman

CYCLE 3 CRITICAL PERSPECTIVE COMPREHENSION, *SEEDFOLKS*

Seedfolks operated as a catalyst or agent to bring together folks in an economically challenged, urban, extensively multicultural neighborhood. As different members of this neighborhood began talking to each other while they worked in the garden, they began breaking stereotypes they held of one another, trusting each other, and even helping each other.

Green Literacy teachers ready students for Discussion Web Strategy with the following steps:

Step 1) Introduce young people to the idea of the neighborhood garden being a catalyst or change agent to bring folks in the neighborhood together.

Step 2) Young people write their thoughts about the following question: Do you feel your neighborhood could use such a catalyst to bring folks together?

Afterwards, the teacher requests students to consider different sides of this issue before drawing conclusions by using a Discussion Web (Alvermann, 1991). This strategy uses a graphic display to scaffold students' thinking about the ideas they contribute.

The two sides of this issue may take some thinking and reflection on the part of young people. Students may also want to draw from the text concerning their thinking about the two positions. Taking the "No" position, young people come up with ways their neighborhood is cohesive and supportive of different kinds of people or that there is no value in such cohesion, so there is no need for such a catalyst. This is an approach that elicits deep thinking about their own neighborhoods and their beliefs about people working together. When taking the "Yes" position, young people develop ideas concerning what the benefits of a neighborhood catalyst or project may be. The Conclusion part of the process has young people in the small group come to some kind of consensus, though if one member dissents, a minority opinion can be voiced during the final sharing.

DISCUSSION WEB TEACHING STRATEGY STEPS:

1. Students work in pairs to generate the pros and cons of the question on the Discussion Web: *Do you think your neighborhood could use a catalyst to bring folks together?*

2. Students may use keywords and phrases to express their ideas and need not fill all of the lines. They should, however, push themselves to list an equal number of pro and con reasons on the web.

3. Partners combine into groups of four to compare responses and work toward consensus on a conclusion as a group. The Green Literacy teacher explains that it is okay to disagree with other members of the group, but to keep an open mind while listening to others. (Dissenting views may be offered during the whole-class discussion.)

After each group has reached a conclusion and written it on their Discussion Web, the teacher provides each group with three or four minutes to decide which of all the reasons best supports the group's conclusion. A spokesperson reports the consensus conclusion and may also give any dissenting opinions.

DISCUSSION WEB FOR *SEEDFOLKS*

Overall Question to Consider: Do you think your neighborhood could use a catalyst to bring folks together?

* No. My neighborhood is a cohesive and supportive group of people.

(Young people complete their support of this statement.)

* Yes. There is an "each man/ woman/ family for itself" mentality in my neighborhood, so such a catalyst would be helpful.

(Young people complete their support of this statement.)

COMMENTARY ON THE FILM *JANE'S JOURNEY*, BIOGRAPHY OF A HUMAN & PRIMATE FRIENDSHIP

Lorenz Knauer's one hour and 51 minute film, *Jane's Journey*, focuses on primatologist and environmental activist Jane Goodall. Goodall dedicated her life to the natural world and its preservation. In particular, Jane focused much of her time and research on primates such as chimpanzees. Jane believes in human and primate friendship. This biography is a subtle call to arms for animal and human rights. We consider this a biography of a human and primate friendship. As the film tells the story of Jane Goodall, so the story of primates unfolds. Along with this film readers are introduced to Jane's Roots and Shoots organization, which connects people and their advocacy for a sustainable planet.

The film starts with the 75-year-old Goodall reflecting on her life. Through her recollections and film footage, we meet the girl who went to Tanzania to commune with the chimpanzees. These brief glimpses paint a fascinating portrait of Goodall's early career, marriages, and motherhood. The film describes a major life shift when Jane, in 1986, opened the Jane Goodall Institute, which empowers people to make positive differences in the lives of all living things, including primates. Watching the film builds up young people's awareness toward different organizations connecting through the theme of helping the planet.

TEACHING STRATEGIES FOR *JANE'S JOURNEY*
CYCLES 1 AND 2 SIMPLE COMPREHENSION AND
CRITERIA COMPREHENSION: *JANE'S JOURNEY*
While watching Jane's Journey take notes on what Jane did, how others supported her and the projects she talked about.

CYCLE 3 CRITICAL PERSPECTIVE COMPREHENSION
JANE'S JOURNEY
Free write on connections to *Jane's Journey*

CYCLES 1 AND 2 SIMPLE COMPREHENSION AND
CRITERIA COMPREHENSION: *JANE'S JOURNEY*

While watching the DVD, *Jane's Journey*, young people jot responses to the following open-ended questions about Jane Goodall, her projects and the people who supported her:

* What does Jane do?
* Who were the people in the different parts of Jane's life that supported her as a child, when she went to Tanzania to study chimpanzees in her 20s, as she conducted the many studies of the chimpanzees, and finally during her life as an activist?
* List projects that she talked about.

After watching the film, young people discuss their responses. Then in small groups, students complete the chart below. Afterward, they engage in large group discussion centering on how each of the projects helped people or the natural world or both. In the next class students will come back to their ideas. Students gather again in small groups. Students discuss what led Jane later in her life to devote herself to activism. Groups make a list of reasons, then compare their lists in the whole group.

Jane's Life and People who Supported Her
A River Ran Wild by Lynn Cherry

* What happened in Jane's life? Events in Jane Goodall's Life
* Who helped Jane? People who supported Jane
* Results of Jane Goodall's efforts and the people who supported her.

Cycle 3: Critical Perspective Comprehension
Jane's Journey

Building on prior activities and knowledge, students integrate their ideas through the strategy called Free Write. Students Free Write on the following:

* What personal connections do you make to the ideas in *Jane's Journey*?
* How do you connect with animals?
* In what ways do you share with Jane and her friendship with animals?
* What are some animal friendship ideas and projects you might like to try?

Free Write Tips

Free writing is a simple process that is the basis for other discovery techniques. Basic free writing follows these student guidelines:

- Write nonstop for a set period of time (5–15 minutes).
- Do not make corrections as you write.
- Keep writing, even if you have to write something like, "I don't know what to write."
- Write whatever comes into your mind.
- Do not judge or censor what you are writing.

Using Free Writing in conjunction with group discussion on a single text and/or digital media and then later adding ideas drawn from additional texts and/or digital media is one way students integrate their big picture ideas. It is also another way to hone in on skills set within the CCSS. Teachers who use Free Write often remark student ideas jell over time. Many times with the aid of Free Write, students articulate their ideas and feelings more clearly.

COMMENTARY BIOGRAPHY OF KID EMPOWERED MOVEMENT:
TED Talk by Kiran Bir Sethi
https://www.ted.com/talks/kiran_bir_sethi_teaches_kids_to_take_charge
How do young people become leaders? How do young people inspire other young people to become leaders? How can change be "infectious"? In this 9 minute *TED Talk*, school principal, Mrs. Kiran Bir Sethi, in India addresses these questions by telling how the young people who attend Riverside School embark on solving a local problem and

inspire change within themselves and their school that ultimately leads to other young people becoming empowered throughout all of India. We consider this digital media a biography of Kids-Centered Movement because one story interweaves with another and all of the stories about the children's activism connect together through the I Can motto. Kiran Bir Sethi also adds the We Can motto that we embrace.

Through the 6 Step Process, the young people in the *TED Talk* move to an I Can! /We Can! winning attitude about their accomplishments. Their successes ignite a desire to work together in groups. These steps outlined below offer Green Literacy teachers and students a guideline to participate in the I Can!/We Can! Process.

I CAN!/ WE CAN! 6 STEP PROCESS
Step 1: Listen
Adults, teachers, parents listen to young people's ideas and encourage them to think deeply and critically. "Listening to young people validates them and is particularly important", says Mrs. Kiran Bir Sethi, for then the young people feel supported and confident.

Step 2: Become Aware
Young people become aware of a local problem of interest they would like to solve. For example, in the *TED Talk*,

Riverside young people wanted their town to stop child labor since in their city many children worked long hours at little pay and did not attend school.

Step 3: Enable
Young people brainstorm and critically discuss what actions will solve the problem. With the support and guidance of adults, young people determine their course of action.

Step 4: Empower
As young people implement their plan, they see direct changes on the local problem they wanted to change. They recognize how their efforts pay off with sustainable solutions. For example, in the *TED Talk* young people canvassed their town and talked with local community members about child labor laws, which led to street children enrolling in school.

Step 5: Reflect
Young people reflect on what they learned and accomplished. Their reflection enables them to make changes where needed to better their solutions. Also, reflections lend to inner personal awareness about self and the group dynamics of working together.

Step 6: Share
From these actions, many young people share their success with other young people.

In the *TED Talk* young people call their process I Can/ We Can. They shared their ideas with children in neighboring towns and states until all of India's school children were invited to create their own I Can/We Can projects and shared them with others. Some example projects related to the environment included safe drinking water and recycling.

Cycles 1 and 2 Simple Comprehension and Criteria Comprehension Kiran Bir Sethi's *TED Talk*

Discussion concerning how to create the I Can bug
Free write on projects they would like to pursue

Cycle 3 Criteria Comprehension and Critical Perspective Comprehension: Kiran Bir Sethi's *TED Talk*

Take one idea, something that students are bothered by, and work on it for one week. Free write, discuss and reflect.

Cycles 1 and 2 Simple Comprehension and Criteria Comprehension Kiran Bir Sethi's *TED Talk*

In the beginning of the *TED Talk*, Sethi declared ideas are worth spreading, especially ideas of young people. Through a process of adults listening and young people taking action, she says everyone who participated became infected with the "I CAN" bug, where they are empowered to make social changes in their local environment. Their actions provoked changes, not only in the projects they picked but also in the attitudes of the people who lived in their town. Sethi explains in the *TED Talk* that Ahmedabad became the first child-friendly city, telling its young people they were important and their opinions and actions mattered. Setting the foundation for empowerment takes time and discussion, allowing student voice and choice.

After watching the *TED Talk*, bring students into a discussion using the following critical thinking questions. Teacher facilitates dialogue. Students find personal connections.

How were the young people infected with the "I Can / We Can Bug"? How did the adults guide the young people?

What would happen to our class if we were infected with the "I Can/ We Can"?

How would the adults guide us?

What did Ahmedabad do to become the first child-friendly city, telling all of the young people in the city, "You Can"?

If your school community did the same as Ahmedabad, how would you feel?

What were the specific projects young people made?

What are projects you want to do?

From this discussion and in conjunction with the work done for the digital media *Jane's Journey*, have students write a second, follow-up Free Write about ideas they would like to implement. Then brainstorm as a class or in small groups ideas they would like to implement concerning environmental stewardship in their local community. In this way, the teacher supports students in exploring their own ideas of projects they would like to pursue.

Cycle 3 Criteria Comprehension and Critical Perspective Comprehension: Kiran Bir Sethi's *TED Talk*

Kiran challenges all the viewers to take one idea, something that bothers them, and work on it for one week. In the *TED Talk* children across India had such ideas as recycling, water improvement, and adult literacy. With young people committed to one idea, she suggests that one billion lives will change. Students create their own One Week, One Idea Project. Use the graphic to help identify an idea and the steps to take.

One Week, One Idea

* What is your idea?
* What problem do you want to change into a possibility?
* What are the steps you can take to change the problem into a possibility?

Once the class has the ideas and the steps, they put into action their One Week, One Idea Plan. During the week, students keep a journal about the project's process. When the week finishes, students reflect on the their process using the following questions, first in a Free Write, then in a large class discussion:

* How does working together on projects unify your class?
* How did you shift your perspective of problem to possibility when you decided on your project?
* How does shifting your perspective change the way you think and act about where you live?

Commentary on Different Types Environmental Leaders:
Seedfolks, Jane's Journey & Kiran Bir Sethi's TED Talk

Environmental leadership does not resemble a cookie cutter. Rather, environmental leadership encourages various forms of commitment, idea, and action that may intertwine for the best possible solution for that local community. In the novel *Seedfolks*, the digital media *Jane's Journey*, and Kiran Bir Sethi's *TED Talk*, young people engage in different types and levels of environmental leadership. All began with actions of empowerment in their local community. Second, they fostered strong connections with nature. Third, they solved problems creatively and collectively.

Most importantly, the young people represented in these texts/digital media understood when their community unites, problems transform into possibilities, so that sustainable solutions come about.

With a close reading of the novel *Seedfolks*, young people recognize that the character Kim planted the first seed, which prompted others in her neighborhood to plant and tend the garden. Neighbors contributed their time, talent, and efforts in their own way to change the landscape of the neighborhood. This type of environmental leadership is Distributed Leadership; people learn to trust each other and embark on a project. The roles are collaborative; there is no assumed or selected leader among the group.

In *Jane's Journey*, Jane Goodall, through her organization Roots and Shoots, becomes an international meta-leader. With her organization, she raises consciousness about species extinction, impoverished peoples and their connections to environmental degradation through over-consumption. Meta-leadership such as that provided by Jane Goodall centers on strategically linking the efforts of different organizations. Through linking there is guidance, direction, and momentum across organizational lines. This gives a shared course of action and purpose among people may who appear to be doing very different work. Jane and her organization inspire many diverse people across the globe to take leadership roles.

The young people within Kiran Bir Sethi's *TED Talk* use Critical Leadership to examine and solve community challenges. Critical Leaders are sometimes found in schools and community centers. Critical Leadership based on Critical Pedagogy focuses on questioning power relationships and their impact on the local environment, moving toward the global. The leader is a facilitator. She listens, validates, and prompts a small group of individuals to critically discuss issues they deem important. After dialogue and inquiry, action items are created and implemented, and ultimately lead to empowerment for the members in the small group.

ENVIRONMENTAL LEADERSHIP

Environmental leadership centers on moving from problem to possibility by implementing the best type of leadership for a specific situation. The books and digital media in the section focused on the following environmental leadership styles.

* **Distributed Leadership** (*Seedfolks*): People learn to trust each other and embark on a project. The roles are collaborative; there is no assumed or selected leader among the group.
* **Meta-leadership** (*Jane's Journey*): centers on strategically linking the efforts of different organizations. Linking provides guidance, direction, and momentum across organizational lines. This gives

a shared course of action and purpose among people who may do different work.

* **Critical Leadership** (Kiran Bir Sethi *TED Talk*): based on Critical Pedagogy, focuses on questioning power relationships and their impact on the local environment, moving toward the global. The leader is a facilitator who leads the group to develop do-able projects initiated by the group members.

COMPARING *SEEDFOLKS*, *JANE'S JOURNEY*, AND KIRAN BIR SETHI'S *TED TALK*

Students compare *Seedfolks*, *Jane's Journey*, and Kiran Bir Sethi's *TED* Talk using the following steps:

1) In small groups, students discuss and determine how these books are similar and/or different in terms of leadership style.
2) They write what is the theme or essential message for each text and digital media.
3) Finally, each group decides which of the three themes or essential messages is the most important to them within their local community/situation. Why do they think so? How do the chosen themes from the books/media connect with their ideas they plan to put into action?

RECOGNIZING CENTRAL THEMES

We recognize there are several themes within each of the books, and student answers will vary. We provide central themes as a reference point for Green Literacy teachers.

> *Seedfolks*: Through working together on a project that promotes earth sustainability, diverse people begin to value and befriend each other.
>
> *Jane's Journey*: An individual commits one's time and efforts to supporting various community projects around the globe and makes a difference toward a sustainable future.
>
> **Kiran Bir Sethi's *TED Talk*:** When young people are listened to, they become aware of ramifications of issues of their choosing and then empowered to take action, and finally to reflect on how to make a greater impact in their local environment.

Discussion will likely bring into play many of the ideas mentioned in the beginning of this Teaching Unit, especially how communities move from environmental problems to possibilities. The themes or messages from the text and media jumpstart dialogue concerning actions students may want to take in order to better their community. For example, if they participated in the One Week One Idea Project, they have more project ideas they would like to implement. Further discussion will draw students into what type of leadership best serves the local project at hand.

We believe that as students engage and empower themselves and others, they begin to recognize and value communicating and interacting in ways they may have not done before. Through this process, it is our hope that students and teachers will create Green Literacy Ideals surrounding environmental leadership and participant buy-in. We advocate young people create Green Literacy Ideals that will best serve a specific purpose and that makes sense to them.

ENVIRONMENTAL LEADERS & STUDENT INITIATED ACTION

In this Teaching Unit, it is our hope that students will be inspired to bring change to their local landscape by working together and using the elements of environmental leadership explored. The following is a set of questions for students to (1) answer individually; (2) share out in small groups, and then (3) come to a consensus in the large group.

- Considering the three different styles of leadership, which style would be more effective for your project and your class? Why?
- What actions need to be taken to create positive connections among classmates, trust, and a "working together" spirit?
- How would doing Internet research and working with an international organization such as Roots

and Shoots energize and support your group when you are creating action items?

* How much adult leadership is needed? What role would the adult take? How can you share your "I Can/ We Can" bug with others? How would you advise other young people through this process?
* What Green Literacy Ideals would you create after working with this project?

Through these discussions, students may come up with actions the group wants to pursue that involve leadership, starts where you are, and works in your community to effect change moving from problems to possibility. We strongly suggest that whatever action plans students discuss, they take on research using the Internet and second, students share their projects with a wider audience using technological tools such as blogs and podcasts. In the next section, Investigate & Connect Through Writing, we explore how to extend the discussion into research, writing, and production.

Investigate & Connect through Writing
Adaptable K-5

Environmental leaders know it takes a fortified effort to connect with others. Environmental leaders are flexible and determine the best type of leadership for a specific environmental challenge. They know how to build relationships with others. In this Teaching Unit, we focused on these two thematic questions about environmental leaders: (1) what are the characteristics of an environmental leader and (2) how do young people become environmental leaders? Keeping these questions in mind, we turn toward investigating environmental leadership.

There are many websites young people can use to investigate the two questions. These sites focus on projects spearheaded by many different types of people, including young people. Investigate examples of young people working together on environmental stewardship projects.

Here are a few of our favorite environmental stewardship projects summarized from these websites. Class members use one of these projects for their writing or they find their own favorites.

1. **Youth Activism Projec**t: A non-partisan organization that encourages young people to speak up and pursue lasting solutions to problems they care deeply about while promoting civic engagement. One case of youth working together is the Pelican Island Elementary School. Students in Florida made dozens of presentations to the School Board, the Indian River County Commission, their U.S. Representative, and the Secretary of the U.S. Interior Department to protect the habitat of the scrub jay, an endangered species.

2. **Roots and Shoot.Org:** Wildlife Journaling introduces students to wetlands estuaries and urban

wildlife unit plan, creating scientific nature journals using art and science and outdoor and indoor experiential learning. Youth-created projects offer ideas for local environmental leadership.

3. **The Child in Nature Network**: This organization is designed to connect families and nature through family practices, creating nature rich cities, engaging families in outdoor activities, and engaging change makers from throughout the world. http://www.childrenandnature.org/

Bringing it to the World: Youth Blog & Podcasting Environmental Leadership

Another way to connect to others is through either a blog or a podcast. Classroom blogs and podcasts provide an opportunity for students to write, produce, and use technology to reach authentic audiences beyond their own classmates. Classrooms could partner with another classroom – that classroom could even be on the other side of the world.

Here is a resource for Green Literacy teachers who have not made a podcast before. They get started by going to http://greenliteracy.org/. This website tells you how to develop an MP3 and to make and edit your podcast.

For those who have never blogged, Edublog is a free resource for learning about and setting up classroom blogs. Blogs and podcasts are similar in that they reach a wide audience and give student choice and voice. Remember the following 4 steps of Hot Blogging (Zawlinski, 2009) and/or Hot Podcasting:

1. Bolster Background: Use digital format that fits your research best. Some prefer audio format, others prefer both the video and audio of podcasts, and others prefer the standard blog. One's comfort level and availability of technology is also a factor in choosing technology.

2. Prime the Pump: Have students share initial ideas for extended writing and researching. For example, for the podcast and/or blog about the selections above, students would consider what needs clarification, first impressions of story or characters, connections to self, text, or the world. Young people read/view/listen to their classmates' blogs or podcasts and share classmates' postings (not their own) in class discussions. This approach holds students accountable. They must read and remember peers' ideas from the start of the conversation. Another way that classrooms use blogs or podcasts is as an exchange between two classes. For example, both classes have read *The Mangrove Tree: Planting Trees to Feed Families*, and K-2 students write (or dictate) their connections and "wonderings" concerning the ideas in this book with each other on the blog. Older or more advanced students make a podcast for reading responses.

3. Continue the Conversation: Both in person and through more blogging and/or podcasting, young people synthesize their ideas across the different texts: *Seeds of Change*, *A River Ran Wild*, *She's Wearing a Dead Bird on Her Head!*, and *Dickey Downy*. Students will include others' discussion points as well as new thinking and will move beyond simple recall.

4. Make Multiplicity Explicit: Young people will encounter classmates' differing viewpoints. Such exposure supports students' consideration of various beliefs and positions. As young people distinguish a variety of opinions, they identify the importance of supporting one's point of view clearly. Consider *Seedfolks*. Written and spoken dialogue about the voices in different Teaching Units will encourage students to reflect on differing beliefs and positions of the young people blogging as well as the different voices in the Teaching Unit. Also students may dramatize events in *Jane's Journey* and record them digitally for video podcasts.

Green Heroes K-5 Thematic Teaching Units
References

Alvermann, D. E. (1991). The discussion web: A graphic aid to learn across the curriculum. *The Reading Teacher, 45,* 92–99.

Carson, R. (1962, renewed 1990). Silent spring: The classic that launched the environmental movement. New York: Mariner.

Zawlinski, L. (2009). HOT blogging: A framework for blogging to promote higher order thinking. *The Reading Teacher 62*(8), 650-661. doi: 10.1598/RT.62.8.3

APPENDIX A: GREEN LITERACY THEORY

● ● ●

GREEN LITERACY TAKES A CRITICAL STANCE

GREEN LITERACY IS PART OF critical pedagogy, which emphasizes that teachers and students can take a critical stance that looks at power relationships toward any text—from fairy tales to newspaper articles and everything in between. For example, fourth graders could read *Cinderella*, take a critical stance, and ask who had power over Cinderella's life in the beginning of story. Why allow the stepmother and her daughters to order Cinderella around and make her into a servant rather than as a respected member of the household as her two stepsisters? The fourth graders may talk about experiences in their "blended families" to understand the plight of Cinderella and the family dynamics in the beginning of the story. In the Cinderella story, the teacher focused on family power issues, while in Green Literacy the power considered is related to human impact on the earth.

In Green Literacy Practice, teachers and their students take a critical stance in multiple ways by bearing in mind power relationships and their connection to environmental justice themes. Power entails different forms: position, physical strength/control, money, and skills and competence, including literacy abilities. They take a critical stance when they ask questions that lead to an analysis of voices and perspectives, both present and excluded in the text. They take a critical stance when they consider whose perspective is credible and support their reasoning. They take a critical stance when they reflect on who has power in the situation and how others may be empowered.

We view the work of Ira Shor (1992), a leading exponent of Critical Pedagogy, as a guide to create critical stance. The information, research, and analysis of environmental themes that students and their teachers undertake in Series 1-4 achieve what Shor calls, "Habits of thought, reading, writing, and speaking which go beneath surface meaning, first impressions, dominant myths, official pronouncements, traditional clichés, received wisdom, and mere opinions, to understand the deep meaning, root causes, social context, ideology, and personal consequences of any action, event, object, process, organization, experience, text, subject matter, policy, mass media, or discourse" (p. 129).

Through the themes found in our thematic teaching units, young people take a critical stance when they come to realize that our natural resources are limited and that a sense of valuing place and earth stewardship is as important as race, class, and gender to our identity. Young people begin to formulate a critical stance when they grasp that there are clear winners and losers in the old ways of mining, polluting, and using up the global commons of air, water, fossil fuels, and forests, and not realizing that we are dependent on nature for our very lives. Rather, Green Literacy themes within our thematic teaching units encourage young people to be winners through taking a critical stance by engaging in themes and determining their local and global consequences.

Rooted in the work of Paulo Freire (1970), Green Literacy advocates that literacy instruction empowers people to make changes needed both in their lives and in the power structures in which they live. Freire reminds us that literacy education is never neutral: the way literacy skills are taught can be liberating and empowering through a critical stance.

In each of the Series we encourage teachers and students to develop a critical stance through engaging in our commentaries about environmental themes and the books and digital media within in the Green Literacy suggested readings and viewings

GREEN LITERACY FRAMEWORK WITH FOUR AGREEMENTS

Green Literacy Framework has four agreements or premises underlying classroom interactions so that students and their teachers have in-depth dialogues concerning the many aspects of environmental stewardship.

As stated in the Introduction, we define Green Literacy as a way of teaching that supports students in critical dialogue, systemic thinking, and meaningful responding to our human impact on the natural world. In other words, Green Literacy is a practice of teaching that develops in-depth thinking, dialoging, and responding to our relationship to the environment through using multiple texts and digital media as catalysts. Green Literacy is considered a branch of Critical Pedagogy, sometimes called critical literacy, which encourages young people to consider power issues. In Green Literacy's case, students and teachers engage in power issues that surround environmental themes.

Considering the definition of Green Literacy, we developed a framework with four agreements or premises underlying classroom interactions so that students and their teachers have in-depth dialogues concerning the many aspects of environmental stewardship. Without these agreements we believe these conversations are unlikely to occur. As we worked in classrooms we saw that with a disciplined commitment to these agreements, over time and practice, students and teachers engage in in-depth dialogues concerning environmental justice that often lead to student-initiated action. The four agreements students and teachers practice over time and space are the following:

Agreement 1: *Understands knowledge of the world advances reading words* (Freire, 1970): What Green Literacy students know about the world, especially power relationships, advances "reading words," especially comprehension skills. Through reading, dialoguing and critical thinking, students can create a depth of meaning and the significance of eco-social context on themes that matter.

Agreement 2: *Generates themes from personal connections to various texts and other media*: Green Literacy students generate environmental themes from the connections they make to books and digital media to promote critical discussions that examine dominant myths, for example, "Natural resources are limitless." Discussions around generative themes in Green Literacy promote students holding many perspectives in mind, coming up with "a bigger story" rather than fragments of certain issues.

Agreement 3: *Facilitates an open and non-authoritarian stance* (Shannon, 1990): Green Literacy students share power and responsibility with the Green Literacy teacher. Green Literacy students exchange ideas and opinions, which fuel more expressions that ultimately lead to the class pursuing their ideas for classroom or school-at-large projects and activities. The Green Literacy student takes initiative, within constraints of time, resources, school policy, and common sense.

Agreement 4: *Questions power relationships* (Shor, 1992): Both Green Literacy students and teachers realize that society is made of contending forces and interests. Green Literacy students and teachers artfully advance questions to examine viewpoints of characters and authors that lead to analysis of voices and perspectives present or excluded, whose perspective is credible, who has power in situations, and what that power entails, that is, skills and competence, physical strength, money, or position.

In the Introduction, we stated that authors and readers are influential people who have the capacity to perpetuate or challenge particular perceptions of the world, including issues of environmental justice. This occurs over time and space through multiple critical dialogues. Much in-depth dialogue needs to happen, particularly around the credibility and validity of differing ideas concerning protecting the environment and humans for some consensus to be reached. Thus we have seen that in this on-going process using the four agreements, students and teachers generate what we call Green Literacy Ideals.

Next we turn to the importance and the creating of Green Literacy Ideals, part of the Green Literacy Process.

GREEN LITERACY IDEALS

Green Literacy Ideals are a set of shared values about our relationship with the living world. Collectively, each classroom defines their Green Literacy Ideals through a process of discussion and evaluation of environmental themes.

Every young person has a right to his or her opinion, multiple perspectives, and embedded values. Green Literacy students wrestle with and change their opinions, even their values, as they read, view, and dialogue about environmental social justice issues. We encourage young people to investigate multiple perspectives with a self-correction strategy and discourage easy, quick answers to complex problems. Young people identify problematic arguments by carefully reflecting on diverse points of view and how such perspectives advance differing "lenses." While this strategy works over time, it may not occur in one lesson or even one unit of teaching. Where competing visions may seem equally valid at first, over the long haul some perspectives will prove more robust, have more explanatory authority, or begin to "make sense." As a young person grapples more intensely with the environmental issue, some insights take on increased significance. Evaluating differing perceptions in an in-depth way ultimately involves thinking through what a young person prizes, particularly in the big picture (Vanquez, Tate, & Harste, 2013). The assessment a young person finally arrives at is embedded in *a set of ideals*, which we call Green Literacy Ideals.

We define Green Literacy Ideals as a set of shared values about our relationship with the living world. Collectively, each classroom defines their Green Literacy Ideals through a process of discussion and evaluation of environmental themes. Coming to a consensus takes time and due diligence, but the results have the possibility of radically changing the way young people think, dialogue, and act when faced with higher-level thinking challenges, such as those surrounding environment.

We, the authors, have conversed about complex environmental issues with each other as well as using Green Literacy strategies with teachers and students. Through these discussions, we developed shared ideals concerning the environment and our human connection to it. On many occasions our ideals emerged over time within our conversations and reflections, which ultimately would determine our actions. We put aside time and space to explore, create, and name our Green Literacy Ideals. We respected that although we created these ideals, we were not bound by them but could modify them if our perspectives shifted. Our Green Literacy Ideals gave us a unique and shared premise to evaluate environmental issues both locally and globally.

In light of this, we provide our Green Literacy Ideals to serve as an example, so that teachers and students may be inspired to create their own. In addition, we also illustrate classrooms creating Green Literacy Ideals in the two vignettes within Creating a Green Literacy Classroom One, for both lower grades and middle grades. Also, developing Green Literacy Ideals will occur in each of the Series Thematic Teaching Units.

Our Green Literacy Ideals

We believe humans are interdependent with other animals and plants on the Earth.

We believe humans must protect the diversity of nature, which includes human nature.

We believe individual species of animals and plants need a suitable ecological system large enough to survive and thrive.

We believe natural resources need to be used carefully and wisely.

We believe in solving problems systematically.

Young people facilitated by their teachers during the Green Literacy practice craft Green Literacy Ideals over time. We strongly recommend students and their teacher develop their Green Literacy Ideals as they work with environmental themes within Green Literacy. We have found that classrooms that displayed their Green Literacy Ideals often had a stronger student buy-in and were more able to incorporate and articulate the ideals into their thinking. We also suggest that as classrooms create Green Literacy Ideals they remain open to changing them.

Green Literacy's 3 Cycles of Comprehension

3 Cycles of Comprehension is a system of comprehension used to explore concepts in texts and media that ultimately leads students into deep critical thinking, talking, and, one hopes, action.

We developed a system of comprehension that incorporates 3 Cycles of Comprehension, which are Cycle 1 Simple Comprehension, Cycle 2 Criteria Comprehension, and Cycle 3 Critical Perspective Comprehension. We advocate 3 Cycles of Comprehension to explore the ideas in texts and digital media within Green Literacy Thematic Teaching Units. Our 3 Cycles of Comprehension are progressive and ultimately lead students into deep critical thinking, talking, and. optimistically, action.

Definitions of the 3 Cycles of Comprehension

Cycle 1: Simple Comprehension occurs when young people retell or summarize the story/nonfiction text or digital media, including when they make inferences about what the author wrote.

Cycle 2: Criteria Comprehension occurs when young people support their thinking about the story/nonfiction text or digital media with criteria either prompted by the teacher or from their own thinking.

Cycle 3: Critical Perspective Comprehension occurs when young people engage in the story/nonfiction text or digital media that becomes less an end in itself than a doorway through which they explore the social world and their relationship to it. This includes both explicit and implicit perspectives and characters debating different sides of issues, as well as valuing and developing assumptions and beliefs that make sense to the young people. Critical Perspective Comprehension also includes systems thinking, that is, thinking which concerns how one event is related to or is caused by other events and involves solving complex problems.

Cycle 1: Simple Comprehension

Simple Comprehension is the first layer or cycle of teaching and learning. Green Literacy students focus on understanding the text, that is, to restate or summarize the story, including making inferences about what the author wrote. In Simple Comprehension, students identify literary devices used when talking about a fiction or nonfiction book such as scene, character, plot, climax, and theme, as well as identifying the main idea and supporting details of the text. In Common Core State Standards (CCSS) parlance, Simple Comprehension is the beginning of "close reading" needed for college and career readiness. In Green Literacy's practice this is the task in Simple Comprehension where the focus is on understanding rather than agreement, since understanding what the author says does not require the reader's agreement.

We offer a study by Albers, Vander-Zander, and Felderman (2008) that illustrates Simple Comprehension and shows the need to move into the next two cycles of comprehension. In this study Albers et al. found that pre-service teachers and 5th graders were able to read and comprehend with Simple Comprehension but had little success at identifying the underlying tacit messages encountered in our consumer culture. Investigators showed both groups a Wal-Mart ad that introduced a new Barbie clothing collection. The Wal-Mart ad displayed three smiling girls dressed in various shades of pink confidently marching down a fashion runway. Barbie doll clothing and complementary accessories lined the margins of the ad. Both the pre-service teachers and the 5th graders talked about affluence, happiness, and fashion, which was what the designers of this ad portrayed. From a Green Literacy perspective, both the pre-service teachers and the 5th graders reached Simple Comprehension of the ads, including making inferences about what the producers of the ad portrayed.

The graphic designer sold not only a product but also a lifestyle, meaning valuing one race and class over another, and the idea that to be a good person one needs such things as a Barbie doll. Neither group attempted to unpack the larger messages about a consumerist culture that the numerous elements of this ad connected to send the viewer. The Albers et al. study in which neither pre-service teachers nor 5th graders saw the projection of a consumerist culture in ads which they watched leads us to consider that most citizens, which include young people in the "first world," have their privileged "hands in the cookie jar" (Leland & Harste, 2000). The "cookie jar" is the consumerist lifestyle that most of us in the "first world' live out daily and those in developing countries may not. We advocate developing an awareness of how young people's habits are complicit in maintaining the systems that drastically endanger the world's limited natural resource base. Our experience indicates that as young people work with Green Literacy, this kind of eco-awareness grows.

This example shows the need to advance students from Cycle 1 Simple Comprehension into the next two cycles of comprehension, Cycle 2 Criteria Comprehension and Cycle 3 Critical Perspective Comprehension.

CYCLE 2: CRITERIA COMPREHENSION

We define Criteria Comprehension as when young people support their thinking about the story/nonfiction text or digital media with criteria either prompted by the teacher or from their thinking. Young people support their ideas drawing from their background knowledge and from the text or media read. This skill of providing support for their ideas from texts read and media viewed is emphasized through many state standards and in the Common Core State Standards and is much emphasized in college course-work. This is the process by which young people extend and expand their schema or knowledge.

CYCLE 3: CRITICAL PERSPECTIVE COMPREHENSION

We define Cycle 3 Critical Perspective Comprehension as when young people engage in the story/nonfiction text or digital media that becomes less an end in itself than a doorway through which they explore the eco-social world and their relationship to it. Cycle 3 Critical Perspective Comprehension includes both explicit and implicit perspectives and characters debating different sides of issues, as well as valuing and developing assumptions and beliefs that make sense to the young people. The developing of Green Literacy Ideals is part of this process of examining assumptions and beliefs. Cycle 3 Critical Perspective Comprehension also includes systems thinking, that is, thinking which concerns how one event is related to or is caused by other events. Systems thinking often embraces structural fixes or solutions that involve changes to a system in order to solve complex environmental issues. We will discuss the impact of both systems thinking and structural fixes in their own section.

CYCLE 2 CRITERIA COMPREHENSION VS. CYCLE 3 CRITICAL PERSPECTIVE COMPREHENSION

We illustrate the contrast between Cycle 2 Criteria Comprehension and Cycle 3 Critical Perspective Comprehension with two classroom examples drawn from critical literacy studies. After, we provide a Green Literacy classroom vignette that explores consumerism as an environmental issue.

The classroom examples that distinguish between Cycle 2 Criteria Comprehension and Cycle 3 Critical

Perspective Comprehension concern conversations about the bombardment of advertisements, which profoundly influence and ultimately accelerate young people's participation in a consumerist culture. The first study is a classic in critical literacy. The second is more recent. Both studies look at framing young people and their caregivers as differing levels of eco-aware consumers. Most young people as well as some adults tend not to recognize how texts position readers and endow them with identities, in this case as eco-aware consumers. These studies indicate the need for teachers to raise young people into social critique and questioning that interrogates texts in terms of "frames" (Lakoff, 2004) or cultural models (Gee, 1996).

The classic critical literacy study by Shotka (1960) describes a teacher using critical reading, which in Green Literacy we call Cycle 2 Criteria Comprehension. Shotka asked first graders to examine two central questions: 1) What is a home? and 2) What is a community? Through a series of lessons, children compared and contrasted their home experiences with the experiences of children in their textbooks. They recognized similarities: the textbook children play with one another and attend school, and families have people who help them, such as doctors and mailmen. Noted were some differences the students point out such as children in the textbooks always looked clean and happy, and their houses were bigger and prettier than those of the readers. Prompted to explain these distinctions, the children revealed the author and illustrator "couldn't think of making the children look dirty . . . and want the pictures and the stories to be happy [because] children didn't like sad stories" (Shotka, 1960, p. 301). Thus when invited to read critically, that is to support their thinking with criteria around how their life differed from what they saw in the pictures, these students explained why authors and illustrators chose certain representations of the world. The first graders were asked to support their ideas or give criteria for them, which Green Literacy calls Cycle 2 Criteria Comprehension, the second cycle of comprehension.

Green Literacy Process takes readers one more comprehension cycle beyond Shokta's study into Cycle 3 Critical Perspective Comprehension, where these readers would then consider social critique or look at models or points of view. We offer an example that altered the students' focus and eco-awareness into Cycle 3 Critical Perspective Comprehension. Luke, Comber, and O'Brien (1996) depicted a first grade teacher who invited her class to read and analyze how catalogs promoting and selling Mother's Day gifts portrays mothers. Students read the catalogs and interviewed each other using the following questions: How are the mothers in the catalogs similar to and different from real mothers? What mothers are not included in the catalogs? Where do children get the money to buy presents? Why do the catalog producers go through all this trouble to make sure people know what is available? The teacher-directed dialogue led children to realize that their mothers of differing cultural and social class perspectives were not represented in the catalogs. The students then interviewed their own and other mothers in the community about what Mother's Day meant to them. As a result, students revised their concepts of Mother's Day. They perceived that Mother's Day was less about buying gifts and more about sharing time with or helping their mothers in some way. In this way, young people considered the social context of Mother's Day by questioning mothers, and in doing so recognized the difference between media and real life portrayals of Mother's Day.

Thus, in the Cycle 3 Critical Perspective Comprehension Mother's Day example (Luke, et al., 1996), the teacher initiated a discussion about the catalog (the text) and then the children interviewed their own and others' mothers. The findings impelled the children to perceive a point of view that contrasted from the perspective of mothers as the consumer catalog portrayed. Exploring and investigating topics or issues with Cycle 3 Critical Perspective Comprehension is particularly important for young people to become empowered to act on their beliefs. We include in the teaching of Cycle 3 Critical Perspective Comprehension instances where young people and their teacher consider how they *value* or see as ideal certain characteristics of a text, character or person, or point of view. In the teaching illustration above, the students realized that some mothers tend to value restful times and being together more than receiving physical objects.

In Cycle 3 Critical Perspective Comprehension, we also include instances where young people use literacy skills for activism to make the world a better place. For example, in the teaching illustration above, suppose the class decided to write a short Readers' Theatre about what they learned by analyzing the catalog and interviewing real mothers about what mothers *really* want from children on Mother's Day and then presented this Readers' Theatre to kindergarteners. This activism using literacy skills would educate kindergarteners.

Cycle 3 Critical Perspective Comprehension as noted in Green Literacy's 3 Cycles of Comprehension proves advantageous for 21st century students' need to realize that each author presents a belief and wants readers to believe it also. Critical literacy theorist Shannon (1995) advocates that educators develop a language of critique with their students to shift their thinking beyond commonplace understandings. One way to develop such a language of critique is by asking students to consider differing perspectives. Cognitive linguist Lakoff's (2004) work called for a precise kind of language study that interrogates texts in terms of "frames" or what Gee, also a linguist, calls cultural models (Gee, 1996). These "frames" position readers in specified ways and endow them with certain identities while reading and analyzing a text. Lakoff defined frames as "mental structures that shape the way we see the world . . . the goals we seek, the plans we make, the way we act" (p. xv).

Thus, critical comprehending, or in the case of Green Literacy Cycle 3 Critical Perspective Comprehension, is not simply having different opinions or even recognizing different points of view. Cycle 3 Critical Perspective Comprehension involves the ability to coordinate multiple layers of complexity including systemic thinking and determining a stance that is *credible* (Sensoy & DiAngelo, 2012, p. 12). Through the understanding of established knowledge, a credible stance brings new evidence to the issues at hand. From a perspective of how children grow in comprehension of material read, soldering connections with their lives and other texts intensifies comprehension, and such correlations journey to opinions. From an academic perspective, knowledge claims must stand up to peer review, scrutiny by those who are specialists in the subject.

In Green Literacy K–5 classrooms, young people wrestle with the process of critical comprehending by supporting their thinking with evidence and considering multiple points of view and systemic thinking. They reflect on, seek deeper clarity, articulate, and discuss an issue with intellectual humility, curiosity, and generosity. The goal is to expand teacher and student knowledge bases and critical thinking, not to protect preexisting opinions. Young people flourish intellectually by critically dialoguing about their opinions, drawing on multiple perspectives and systemic thinking, and conversing about them.

To facilitate deep conversations, multiple texts from many genres are needed. Green Literacy students examine various voices and points of view, which are less likely to happen through reading only one text. In addition, some texts are more profound or provocative than others. Learning through a critical stance includes using texts whose themes enter into vital issues.

Extending these ideas through discussion leads students into an area of thinking called Systems Thinking, where action toward the environment is often made through structural fixes.

We include this kind of comprehending in Cycle 3 Comprehension.

COMPLEXITY OF ENVIRONMENTAL ISSUES AND SYSTEMS THINKING

While young people work with Green Literacy, they quickly realize that environmental challenges are complex and multifaceted. There are no easy solutions to "how to fix" such issues as global warming, dependence on fossil fuels, deforestation, biogenetic foods, air pollution, and the long list that follows without considering the human factor and without realizing such issues are interconnected. For us and for Green Literacy students, the human factor is how we interact both advantageously and adversely with the environment under established systems of law, education, government, medicine, family, and religious organizations. Plus, once young people think about these issues deeply they realize they are related and interconnected.

Green Literacy perceives a system as composed of interrelated parts that affect each other. Natural systems include plants and animals, ocean currents, the climate, the solar system, and ecosystems. Designed systems include machines of all kinds, government agencies, and businesses. The word "system" then refers to many disparate "things" that effect each other's outcome. Environmentalists apply systems thinking by viewing a "problem" as part of an overall system, rather than analyzing specific parts, outcomes, or events.

Therefore, we define Systems Thinking as a set of habits or practices that is based on the belief that the component parts of a system can best be understood in the context of relationships with each other and with other systems, rather than in isolation. Systems Thinking centers on cyclical rather than linear cause and effect and considers the development of long-term unintended consequences, which are often not evident in the short term. Along with most environmentalists, we believe Systems Thinking often leads to possible solutions to complex environmental issues.

Heberlein (2012) writes in *Navigating Environmental Attitudes*, that connecting environmental problems with their complexity, structural fixes, or systemic changes are the most likely to offer a sustainable solution because the changes are systemic and often address the cognitive and technological aspect but in effect demand a reworking of an entire system, including people's attitude.

Systemic changes or structural fixes take some time to absorb and understand. One example of a systemic change that actually occurred is the institution of CAFÉ (Corporate Average Fuel Standards) beginning in 1975 during the Arab Oil Embargo, extended by Congress in 2006, and increased in 2011. The CAFÉ standards are standards that auto makers have to meet where a car or light truck has to have higher gas mileage, that is, the car or light truck can drive farther using less gas. Since cars built under these standards will burn less gas, they will put less global warming pollution into the air. Having US car manufacturers build cars within the CAFÉ standards is a systems change because this affects every car owner within the US and thus has a huge effect on the amount of global warming pollution the US puts into the air. Systems changes usually require support from and decisions made by gatekeepers, in this case, Congress and the President. As the example of raising the CAFÉ standards shows, systemic changes often involve political will—and Green Literacy has young people consider power relationships concerning environmental issues that may lead to creating political will.

Systemic thinking and determining structural fixes are part of the Green Literacy Process. We include it in Cycle 3: Critical Perspective Comprehension. In Cycle 3 we encourage young people to be involved in systemic thinking because we see it as part of teaching critical comprehending. Systems thinking and structural fixes are a focus in Series Four: How can we Cultivate Sustainable Change through Systemic Thinking? In this Series, the Green Literacy teaching unit includes the 20-minute video. "The Story of Stuff," that presents a critical vision of American society that exposes "the connections between a huge number of environmental and social issues." The film calls for creating a more sustainable and just world through systemic changes. Also in Series Four, we introduce Green Literacy young people to the World Peace Game by John Hunter. Playing this game forces young people to broaden and deepen their vision because of the immense complexity and interconnectedness of the world's problems—that is the systemic nature of the environmental issues.

We see the work of Donella Meadows as important considering systems thinking concerning the natural environment. She is one of the most influential environmental thinkers of the 20th century and principal author of *Limits to Growth* (1972) and *Limits to Growth: The Thirty Year Update* (2004) that used computer models to predict how exponential economic and population growth effects finite earth resources. She states that "self-organizing, nonlinear, feedback systems are inherently unpredictable. . . . But there is a message emerging from every computer model we made. Living successfully in a world of systems requires more of us than our ability to calculate. It requires our full humanity—our rationality, our ability to sort out the truth from falsehood, our intuition, our compassion, our vision, and our morality." Further, Meadows emphasizes that "especially in the short term, changes for the good of the whole may sometimes seem to be counter to the interests of a part of the system. It helps to remember that the parts of a system cannot survive without the whole. The long-term health of your liver requires the long-term health of your body, and the long-term interests of sawmills require the long-term health of forests."

CREATING GREEN LITERACY IN-DEPTH DISCUSSIONS

In each of the Green Literacy Series, the Thematic Teaching Units innovatively draw from research on read-aloud discussions that support critical thinking and reading. In the textbox below we explain how Green Literacy Process incorporates this research. We think of the Green Literacy teacher as a facilitator who applies the research to read-alouds, silent reads, and digital media discussions. Teachers with the goal of critical thinking and reading give fewer directives and ask fewer one-answer questions. As the discussion progresses, teachers empower the students to respond to each other's views, not just to the teacher's point of view. Finally, as Green Literacy teachers invite discussion, teachers and students become aware that the common classroom pattern of Teacher Question/Student Answer/ Teacher Evaluate (Cazden, 2001; Eeds & Wells, 1989; McGee, 1995) tends not to support critical response. Green Literacy teachers and their students move away from this pattern.

WHAT GREEN LITERACY TEACHERS DO TO ENHANCE HIGHER LEVEL COMPREHENSION DISCUSSIONS

* Choose high quality literature with complex stories and issues concerning humans' impact on the environment that warrant critical discussion (Hoffman,

Roser, & Battle, 1993; Keene & Zimmerman, 2007; Santoro, Chard, Howard, & Baker, 2008; Sipe, 1998).

* Thoughtfully pre-read the children's literature/digital media as well as related commentaries, and consider thematic connections.

* Determine where in the text/digital media they should stop to talk, what strategies to use as they read the book aloud to engage students in critical dialogue and response and to use these suggestions as models for future lessons.

* Read aloud to the class at least twice to allow higher-level thinking to percolate on the second read. The first read is so that all are "on the same page" and know what the author wrote, that is, Green Literacy's Simple Comprehension (Dennis & Walter, 1995; Martinez & Roser, 1985; McGee & Schickedanz, 2007).

* Engage students in critical dialogue by returning to the idea that, "consciously or unconsciously, when writers write and artists create, they include certain values and perspectives on the world and exclude others" (Crafton, Brennan & Silvers, 2007, p. 513). Also, critical discussions focus on what determines "fair" and "unjust" in stories read and how situations could be changed (Vasquez, 2010).

* Advocate cooperative learning strategies such as Think/Pair/Share or Turn and Talk (Kagan, 1989;

Keene, 2008; Lyman, 1981) as a way to provide each student a chance to explore their ideas on the issue at hand, enriching the whole group talk. When students simultaneously share ideas due to the excitement generated by the conversation, the teacher can refocus on the significant idea in the discussion by saying, "John and Jim, each of you take turns sharing what you said about _____," rather than controlling ways of communication with raising hands (Hoffman, 2011, p. 188).

* Build on student responses by repeating and affirming confirmations, and when there is extensive agreement to act as a "devil's advocate" to bring out alternate points of views if the young people don't do so. In this way the discussion focuses on the interpretive points related to the theme of the text. Also, Green Literacy students build on each other's ideas, rather than presenting unrelated topics (Hoffman, 2011).

REFERENCES

Albers, P., Harste, J. C., Vander-Zanden, S., & Felderman, C. (2008). Using popular culture to promote critical literacy practices. In Y. Kim, V. Risko, D. Comption, D. Dickson, M. Hundley, R. Jimenez, K. Leander, & D. Rowe (Eds.), *57th Yearbook of the National Reading Conference* (pp. 70-83). Oak Creek, WI: NRC.

Alvermann, D. E. (1991). The discussion web: A graphic aid to learn across the curriculum. *The Reading Teacher, 45*, 92–99.

Atwell, N. (1998). *In the middle: New understandings about writing, reading and learning.* Portsmouth, NH: Boynton/Cook.

Calkins, L., Ehrenworth, M., & Lehman, L. (2012). *Pathways to the common core: Accelerating achievement.* Portsmouth, NH: Heinemann.

Cazden, C. (2001). *Classroom discourse: The language of teaching and learning.* Portsmouth, NH: Heinemann.

Coleman, D., & Pimentel, S. (2012). Revised publishers' criteria for the Common Core State Standards in English Language Arts and Literacy, grades K-2. Retrieved from http://www.corestandards.org/

Crafton, L., Brennan, M., & Silvers, P. (2007). Critical inquiry and multiliteracies in a first grade classroom. *Language Arts, 84*(6), 510-518.

Dennis, G., & Walter, E. (1995). The effects of repeated read-alouds on story comprehension as assessed through story retellings. *Reading Improvement, 32*(3), 140-153.

Eeds, M., & Wells, D. (1989). Grand conversations: An exploration of meaning construction in literature study groups. *Research in the Teaching of English, 23*, 4-29.

Freire, P. (1970). *Pedagogy of the oppressed.* New York, NY: Seabury.

Gee, J. (1996). *Social linguistics and literacy: Ideology in discourse* (2nd ed.). New York, NY: Taylor & Francis.

Gewetz, C. (2012). Common standards ignite debate over prereading. *Education Week, 31*(29), 1, 22-23.

Heberlein, T. (2012). *Navigating environmental attitudes.* New York, NY: Oxford University Press.

Hoffman, J. (2011). Co-constructing meaning: Interactive literacy discussions with kindergarten read-alouds. *The Reading Teacher, 65*(3), 183-194. doi: 10.1002/TRTR.01025

Hoffman, J., Roser, N. L., & Battle, J. (1993). Reading aloud in classrooms: From the modal to a "model". *Reading Teacher, 46*(6), 496-505.

Kagan, S. (1989). The structural approach to cooperative learning. *Educational Leadership, 47*(4), 12-15.

Keene, E. O., & Zimmermann, S. (2007). *Mosaic of thought: The power of comprehension strategy instruction* (2nd ed.). Portsmouth, NH: Heineman.

Knapp, M. S. (1995). *Teaching for meaning in high-poverty classrooms.* New York, NY: Teachers College Press.

Lakoff, G. (2004). *Don't think of an elephant: Know your values and frame the debate.* White River Junction, VT: Chelsea Green.

Lawlor, L. (2012). *Rachel Carson and her book that changed the world.* New York, NY: Holiday House.

Leland, C. H., & Harste, J. (2000). Critical literacy: Enlarging the space of the possible. *Primary Voices, 9*(1), 3-7.

Lewison, M., Leland, C, & Harste, J. (2008). *Creating critical classrooms: K- 8 reading and writing with an edge.* New York, NY: Lawrence Erlbaum Associates.

Long, T. W., & Gove, M. K. (2004). How engagement strategies and literature circles promote critical response in a fourth-grade classroom. *The Reading Teacher, 57*(4), 350-361.

Luke, A., Comber, B., & O'Brien, J. (1996). Critical literacies and cultural studies. In M. Anstey & G. Bull

(Eds.), *The literacy lexicon* (pp. 29-44). Melbourne, AU: Prentice-Hall.

Lyman, F. (1981). The responsive classroom discussion. In A. S. Anderson (Ed.), *Mainstreaming digest.* College Park, MD: University of Maryland College of Education.

Martinez, M., & Roser, N. (1985). Read it again: The value of repeated readings during storytime. *Reading Teacher,* *38,* 782-786.

McGee, L. M. (1995). Talking about books with young children. In N. L. Roser & M. G. Martinez (Eds.), *Book talk and beyond: Children and teachers respond to literature* (pp.105-115). Newark, DE: International Reading Association.

McGee, L. M., & Schickedanz, J. A. (2007). Repeated interactive read-alouds in preschool and kindergarten. *Reading Teacher,* *60*(8), 742–751. doi:10.1598/RT.60.8.4

McLaughlin, M., & Overturf, B. J. (2013). *The common core: Teaching K-5 students to meet the reading standards.* Newark, DE: International Reading Association.

Meadows, D., Randers, J., & Meadows, D. (1972) *The limits to growth.* White River Junction, VT: Chelsea Green.

Moser, S. (2007). In the long shadows of inaction: The quiet building of a climate protection movement in the United States. *Global Environmental Politics, 7*(2), 124-144.

National Governors' Center for Best Practice & Council of Chief State School Officers. (2010). Nga.org.

Santoro, L. E., Chard, D. C., Howard, L., & Baker, S. K. (2008). Making the VERY most of read alouds to promote comprehension and vocabulary. *Reading Teacher, 61*(5), 396-408.

Sensoy, O., & DiAngelo, R. (2012). *Is everyone really equal? An introduction to key concepts in social justice education.* New York, NY: Teachers College Press.

Shannon, P. (1990). *The struggle to continue: Progressive reading instruction in the United States.* Portsmith, NH: Heinemann.

Shannon, P. (1995). *Text, lies, & videotape: Stories about life, literacy & learning.* Portsmouth, NH: Heinemann.

Shor, I. (1992). *Empowering education: Critical teaching for social change.* Chicago, IL: University of Chicago Press.

Shotka, J. (1960). Critical thinking in the first grade. In A. J. Mazurkiewicz (Ed.), *New perspectives in reading instruction* (pp. 297-305). New York, NY: Pitman.

Sipe, L. R. (1998). How picture books work: A semiotically framed theory of text-picture relationships. *Children's Literature in Education, 29*(2), 97-108.

Sobel, D. (1996). *Beyond ecophobia: Reclaiming the heart in nature education.* Great Barrington, MA: The Orion Society.

Vasquez, V. M. (2010). *Getting beyond "I like the book." Creating space for critical literacy in K-6 classrooms* (2nd ed.). Newark, DE: International Reading Association.

Vanquez, V. M., Tate, S. L., & Harste, J. C. (2013). *Negotiating critical literacies with teachers: Theoretical foundations and pedagogical resources for pre-service and in-service contexts.* New York, NY: Routledge.

APPENDIX B. COMMON CORE
STATE STANDARDS IN GREEN
LITERACY PRACTICE

● ● ●

THE IMPORTANT WORK OF CRITICAL thinking, discussing, and citing evidence within the text and within digital media is something that occurs in the Green Literacy classroom through thematic teaching units. Green Literacy teachers know that the process of Green Literacy and its thematic teaching units supports the Common Core State Standards (CCSS), as both integrate the goals and skills of English/ language arts, science, and social studies content standards. This intermix of different subjects allows teachers to facilitate real world connections. Equally important, Green Literacy teaching units are arranged thematically, which allows teachers to plunge into several subjects while adhering to the overreaching goal of CCSS that combines Language Arts standards with those of Science and Social Studies. Thus, Green Literacy lends itself well to teaching the CCSS because it is thematically organized and is interdisciplinary in its approach.

We have designed Green Literacy so that teachers feel comfortable and confident that they are implementing skills and goals that align with their district's mandates. Like the CCSS, Green Literacy motivates young people to read more complex texts or view more challenging digital media as they proceed throughout the grades. Green Literacy promotes nonfiction and biography as well as fiction selections and using multiple sources of information presented in diverse formats and media, as does the CCSS. Furthermore, Green Literacy emphasizes the implication and engagement in listening and speaking standards as they correlate to print, digital, and/or personal experience as does CCSS. Moreover, Green Literacy students critically think through environmental themes and cite evidence from print and/or digital multimedia to support their assertions related to texts and speech, both major aspects of the CCSS.

In correlation with the CCSS, Green Literacy supports a 21st century skill, that is, how to read and compose both textually and orally for wide and diverse audiences in a networked world. Reports of young people harming each other online is a reminder that we must help them develop a consciousness of audiences they invoke, ignore, reject, exclude, or deny, that is, adopt critical dispositions. This involves more than blogs and pixel learning, but adopts a modern mindset that prizes collaboration, experimentation,

(Lankshear & Knobel, 2007), a healthy curiosity, a respect for diversity, and an ability to determine the credibility of online sources.

Green Literacy teachers realize that even though a plethora of materials and professional development surround the CCSS, as yet there is no research on effective teaching for all students to achieve these standards, and teachers are the key to improved student learning (Darling-Hammond, 2005). We recognize, as does the National Governors Association in 2010, that the CCSS standards are intended to be a living work: as new and better evidence emerges, the standards will be revised accordingly. As of summer 2014, a large amount of debate is occurring in the media and education circles regarding if and how and when the CCSS should be implemented voluntarily across the 43 states (CCSS website). We trust teachers to apply best practices. We know teachers can skillfully and meaningfully teach above and beyond any standard, CCSS or state standard.

In each of the Green Literacy Series, we emphasize the CCSS Anchor Standards in the thematic teaching units. These Anchor Standards point to overarching goals, not small ones (Valencia & Wixson, 2001, p. 181). Our thematic teaching units are designed to involve young people in dialogue and possibly action concerning big ideas concerning earth stewardship as they meet the CCSS Anchor Standards with more complex material. We understand that teaching the CCSS standards should not be taught alone. Rather, teaching them in isolated lessons, Green Literacy teaching is carefully planned and the content is well-coordinated lessons taught together. As the teacher studies the standards, she can value that the intent is to move young people in their thinking as they read, rather than accumulating a slew of details. Further, young readers need to realize that what an author writes is not *the truth*, but rather *someone's perspective* or their side of the truth (Calkins, Ehrenworkth, & Lehman, 2012).

The Series of Green Literacy's Thematic Teaching Units focus on the following CCSS Anchor Standards and specific CCSS standards:

Anchor Standard Reading Literature: Key Ideas and Details	Specific CCSS *focusing on* 1. Supporting understanding of text; inference 2. Retelling and summarizing, theme 3. Character, setting, events
Anchor Standard Craft and Structure	Specific CCSS *focusing on* 6. Point of View

Chapter 6: Grades K-2 Green Literacy Teaching: Green Heroes
Common Core State Standards K-2
CCSS RI K.1 with prompting and support, ask and answer questions about key details in a text.

CCSS RI 1.1 Ask and answer questions about key details in a text.

CCSS RI 2.1 Ask and answer such questions as who, what, where, when, why, and how to demonstrate understanding of key details in a text.

CCSSS K, 1, 2 Participate in collaborative conversations with diverse partners about kindergarten/ first grade/ 2nd grade topics and texts with peers and adults in small and larger groups.

CCSS SL K.2 Confirm understanding of a text read aloud or information presented orally or through other media by asking and answering questions about key details and requesting clarification if something is not understood.

CCSS SL 1.2 Ask and answer questions about key details in a text read aloud or information presented orally or through other media.

CCSS SL 2.2 Recount or describe key ideas or details from a text read aloud or information presented orally or through other media.

CCSS SL K.3 Ask and answer questions in order to seek help, get information, or clarify something that is not understood.

CCSS SL 1.3 Ask and answer questions about key details in a text read aloud or information presented orally or through other media.

CCSS SL 2.3 Ask and answer questions about what a speaker says in order to clarify comprehension, gather additional information, or deepen understanding of a topic or issue.

Common Core State Standards for Green Heroes
Cycle 1: Simple Comprehension *Seeds of Change*

CCSS RI 3.1 Ask and answer questions to demonstrate understanding of the text, referring explicitly to the text as the basis for answers.

CCSS RI 4.1 Refer to details and examples in a text when explaining what the text says explicitly and when drawing inferences from the text.

Cycle 2: Criteria Comprehension *Seeds of Change*

CCSS RI 3.1 Ask and answer questions to demonstrate understanding of the text, referring explicitly to the text as the basis for answers.

CCSS RL 3.2 Recount stories, determine the central message, and explain how it is conveyed through key details in the text.

CCSS RI 3.7 Use information gained from the words in the text to demonstrate understanding of the text.

CCSS RI 4.1 Refer to details and examples in a text when explaining what the text says explicitly and when drawing inferences from the text.

CCSS RI 4.7 Interpret information and explain how the information contributes to understanding the text.

CYCLE 3: CRITICAL PERSPECTIVE COMPREHENSION
SEEDS OF CHANGE

CCSS RL3.6 Distinguish their own point of view from that of characters.

CCSS RL 4.2 Determine the theme of a story from details in the text; summarize the text.

CCSS RI 5.2 Determine two or more main ideas of a text and explain how they are supported by key details; summarize the text.

CYCLE 1: SIMPLE COMPREHENSION *A RIVER RAN WILD*

CCSS RI 3.1 Ask and answer questions to demonstrate understanding of the text, referring explicitly to the text as the basis for answers.

CCSS RI 4.1 Refer to details and examples in a text when explaining what the text says explicitly and when drawing inferences from the text.

Developing a Timeline

CCSS RI 3.3 Describe the relationship between a series of historical events, using language that pertains to time, sequence, and cause/effect.

CCSS RI 4.3 Explain historical events, including what happened and why, based on specific information in the text.

Cycle 2: Criteria Comprehension *A River Ran Wild*

CCSS RI 3.1 Ask and answer questions to demonstrate understanding of the text, referring explicitly to the text as the basis for answers.

CCSS RI 3.7 Use information gained from the words in the text to demonstrate understanding of the text.

CCSS RI 4.1 Refer to details and examples in a text when explaining what the text says explicitly and when drawing inferences from the text.

CCSS RI 4.7 Interpret information and explain how the information contributes to understanding the text.

Cycle 3: Critical Perspective Comprehension *A River Ran Wild*

CCSS RL3.6 Distinguish their own point of view from that of characters.

CCSS RL 4.2 Determine the theme of a story from details in the text; summarize the text.

CCSS RI 5.2 Determine two or more main ideas of a text and explain how they are supported by key details; summarize the text.

CCSS RI 3.7 Use information gained from the words in the text to demonstrate understanding of the text.

CCSS RI 4.7 Interpret information and explain how the information contributes to understanding the text.

CYCLE 1: SIMPLE COMPREHENSION *SHE'S WEARING A DEAD BIRD ON HER HEAD!*

CCSS RI 3.1 Ask and answer questions to demonstrate understanding of the text, referring explicitly to the text as the basis for answers.

CCSS RI 4.1 Refer to details and examples in a text when explaining what the text says explicitly, and when drawing inferences from the text.

CCSS RI 4.7 Interpret information and explain how the information contributes to understanding the text.

COMPARING *SHE'S WEARING A DEAD BIRD ON HER HEAD!* TO *DICKEY DOWNY*

CCSS RI 3.9 Compare and contrast the most important points and key details presented by two texts on the same (similar) topic.

CCSS RI 4.9 Integrate information from several texts on the same topic in order to write or speak about the subject knowledgeably.

CYCLE 2: CRITERIA COMPREHENSION *SHE'S WEARING A DEAD BIRD ON HER HEAD!*

CCSS RI 3.1 Ask and answer questions to demonstrate understanding of the text, referring explicitly to the text as the basis for answers.

CCSS RI 3.7 Use information gained from the words in the text to demonstrate understanding of the text.

CCSS RI 4.1 Refer to details and examples in a text when explaining what the text says explicitly and when drawing inferences from the text.

CCSS RI 4.7 Interpret information and explain how the information contributes to understanding the text.

CCSS RI 5.2 Determine two or more main ideas of a text and explain how they are supported by key details; summarize the text.

CCSS RI 5.3 Explain the relationships or interactions between two or more events, ideas, or concepts in a historical text based on specific information in the text.

CCSS RL3.6 Distinguish their own point of view from that of characters.

CCSS RL 4.2 Determine the theme of a story from details in the text; summarize the text.

Cycle 3: Critical Perspective Comprehension for *She's Wearing a Dead Bird on Her Head!*

CCSS RI 3.9 Compare and contrast the most important points and key details presented by two texts on the same topic.

CCSS RI 4.9 Integrate information from several texts on the same topic in order to write or speak about the subject knowledgeably.

Comparing *Texts: Seeds of Change, A River Ran Wild,* and *She's Wearing a Dead Bird on Her Head!*

CCSS RI 3.9 Compare and contrast the most important points and key details presented by two texts on the same (similar) topic.

CCSS RI 4.9 Integrate information from several texts on the same topic in order to write or speak about the subject knowledgeably.

CCSS RI 5.9 Integrate information from several texts on the same (or similar) topics in order to speak about the subject knowledgeably.

CCSS RL 4.6 Compare and contrast the point of view from which different stories are narrated.

CCSS RL 4.9 Compare and contrast the treatment of similar themes and topics and patterns of events in stories.

CYCLES 1 AND 2: SIMPLE COMPREHENSION AND CRITERIA COMPREHENSION, SEEDFOLKS

CCSS RI 4.1 Refer to details and examples in a text when explaining what the text says explicitly and when drawing inferences from the text.

CCSS RI 4.6 Interpret information and explain how the information contributes to understanding the text.

CCSS RL 5.1 Quote accurately from a text when explaining what the text says explicitly and when drawing inferences from the text.

CCSS RI 4.7 Interpret information and explain how the information contributes to understanding the text.

CCSS RI 5.2 Determine two or more main ideas of a text and explain how they are supported by key details; summarize the text.

CCSS RL 4.2 Determine the theme of a story from details in the text; summarize the text.

CCSS SL 5.1 Engage effectively in a range of collaborative discussions (one-on-one, in groups, and teacher-led) with diverse partners on grade 5 topics and text, building on others' ideas and expressing their own clearly.

CCSS RI 5.2 Determine two or more main ideas of a text and explain how they are supported by key details; summarize the text.

CCSS RI 4.2 Explain ideas in a text, including what happened and why, based on specific information in the text.

Cycle 3: Critical Perspective Comprehension, *Seedfolks*

CCSS RL 5.1 Quote accurately from a text when explaining what the text says explicitly and when drawing inferences from the text.

CCSS SL 5.1 Engage effectively in a range of collaborative discussions (one-on-one, in groups, and teacher-led) with diverse partners on grade 5 topics and text, building on others' ideas and expressing their own clearly.

CCSS RL3.6 Distinguish their own point of view from that of characters.

RI 4.7 Interpret information and explain how the information contributes to understanding the text.

RL 4.6 Compare and contrast the point of view from which different stories are narrated.

Cycles 1 and 2: Simple Comprehension and Criteria Comprehension: *Jane's Journey*

CCSS RI 4.1 Refer to details and examples in a text when explaining what the text says explicitly and when drawing inferences from the text.

CCSS RI 5.2 Determine two or more main ideas of a text and explain how they are supported by key details; summarize the text.

Cycle 3: Critical Perspective Comprehension
Jane's Journey

CCSS RL 4.2 Determine the theme of a story from details in the text; summarize the text.

CCSS RI 4.7 Interpret information and explain how the information contributes to understanding the text.

CCSS SL 5.1 Engage effectively in a range of collaborative discussions (one-on-one, in groups, and teacher-led) with diverse partners on grade 5 topics and text, building on others' ideas and expressing their own clearly.

Cycles 1 and 2: Simple Comprehension and Criteria Comprehension Kiran Bir Sethi's *TED Talk*

CCSS RI 4.1 Refer to details and examples in a text when explaining what the text says explicitly and when drawing inferences from the text.

CCSS RL 4.2 Determine the theme of a story from details in the text; summarize the text.

CCSS RI 4.7 Interpret information and explain how the information contributes to understanding the text.

CCSS RI 5.2 Determine two or more main ideas of a text and explain how they are supported by key details; summarize the text.

Cycle 3: Criteria Comprehension and Critical Perspective Comprehension: Kiran Bir Sethi's *TED Talk*

CCSS RI 4.1 Refer to details and examples in a text when explaining what the text says explicitly and when drawing inferences from the text.

CCSS RI 4.7 Interpret information and explain how the information contributes to understanding the text.

CCSS RL 5.1 Quote accurately from a text when explaining what the text says explicitly and when drawing inferences from the text.

CCSS RI 5.2 Determine two or more main ideas of a text (or media) and explain how they are supported by key details; summarize the text.

CCSS SL 5.1 Engage effectively in a range of collaborative discussions (one-on-one, in groups, and teacher-led) with diverse partners on grade 5 topics and text, building on others' ideas and expressing their own clearly.

Comparing *Seedfolk, Jane's Journey,* and Kiran Bir Sethi's *TED Talk*

CCSS RI 5.9 Integrate information from several texts (differing things said by classmates) on the same topic in order to write or speak about the subject knowledgeably.

CCSS SL 5.1 Engage effectively in a range of collaborative discussions (one-on-one, in groups, and teacher-led) with diverse partners on grade 5 topics and text, building on others' ideas and expressing their own clearly.

CCSS RI 5.7 Draw on information from multiple print or digital sources, demonstrating ability to locate an answer or to question quickly or to solve a problem efficiently.

References

Calkins, L., Ehrenworth, M., & Lehman, L. (2012). *Pathways to the common core: Accelerating achievement.* Portsmouth, NH: Heinemann.

Coleman, D., & Pimentel, S. (2012). Revised publishers' criteria for the Common Core State Standards in English Language Arts and Literacy, grades K-2. Retrieved from http://www.corestandards.org/

Common Core State Standards in English Language Arts. www.**corestandards**.org/**ELA**-Literacy/

Lankshear, C., & Knobel, M. (2007). *New literacies: Everyday practices and classroom learning.* New York, NY: McGraw Hill.

Valencia, S. W., & Wixson, K. (2001). Inside English/language arts standards: What's in a grade? *Reading Research Quarterly, 36*(2), 202-217.

Darling-Hammond, L. (2005). Teaching as a profession: Lessons is teacher preparation and teacher development. *Phi Delta Kappan*, *87*(3), 237-240.

ABOUT THE AUTHORS

● ● ●

JEN CULLERTON JOHNSON MFA, MED is the author of several books for adults and children including the award winning children's book Seeds of Change (Lee & Low 201). Currently, she teaches at Chicago Public Schools and is a writing professor at Wright College.

Mary K. Gove PhD is an Emeritus professor at Cleveland State University and is co-author of a leading best selling textbook, *Reading and Learning to Read*, which has been in undergraduate and graduate classroom use for twenty years.

GreenLiteracy.org

At our companion website, Greenliteracy.org, we offer exciting student driven, results proven environmental projects, lessons, and references on Green Literacy and its impact on education and our relationship with nature.

Go Deeper with Green Literacy

We host various educator and community professional developments and student engagement workshops. We go deeper with a hybrid format of online and onsite, empowering connections both locally and globally.

Complete your Green Literacy Series

Challenge young people. Invigorate your environmental science program with these amazing titles. Buy directly from our website and put in the code GREEN and receive a 20% discount.

- Series One: How do Young People Become Green Heroes?
- Series Two: How Does Landscape Impact Our Identities?
- Series Three: How Does Extreme Weather Shape Our Communities?
- Series Four: How can we Cultivate Sustainable Change through Systemic Thinking?

GET THE GREENLITERACY.ORG APP

Discover more about how Green Literacy and children's books and digital media are springboards for crucial conversations about our relationship with the nature and environmental stewardship.